High low dolly pepper

Developing music skills with young children

by Veronica Clark

Illustrated by Michael Evans

with a singalong CD of all the songs and stories
performed by Helen Chadwick, Vivien Ellis, Chris Larner,
Missak Takoushian and Stephen Chadwick

SECOND EDITION

A&C Black · London

Second edition 2002
Reprinted in 2006
A&C Black Publishers Ltd
38 Soho Square
London W1D 3HB
© 2002, 1991
A&C Black Publishers Ltd
ISBN 10 0-7136-6345-6
ISBN 13 978-07136-6345-7

Cover illustration by Rachel Fuller
Cover design by Jocelyn Lucas
Inside illustrations © 1991 Michael Evans
Edited by Sheena Roberts
CD produced by Stephen Chadwick and Jane Sebba
Performed by Helen Chadwick, Vivien Ellis, Chris Larner,
Missak Takoushian and Stephen Chadwick

Printed in Great Britain by Martins the Printers Ltd
Berwick on Tweed

A&C Black uses paper produced with elemental chlorine-free
pulp, harvested from managed sustainable forests.

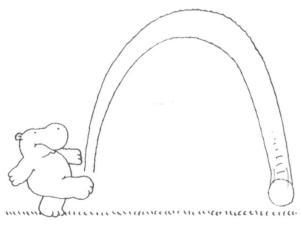

ACKNOWLEDGEMENTS

An old man lives in Lollipop Land © David Moses

Beech leaves, **Rabbit and lark**, **The bogus-boo** and **Slowly the tide** © James
Reeves. From *Complete Poems for Children* by James Reeves (Egmont Children's
Books). Reprinted by permission of the James Reeves Estate.

Engineers by Jimmy Garthwaite from *Puddin' an pie* © 1929 by Harper & Row
Publishers Inc. Copyright renewed 1957 by Merle Garthwaite. Reprinted by
permission of Harper Collins Publishers Inc, New York.

Chinese New Year by Low Siew Poh, © Oxford University Press. Reprinted by
permission.

Granny by Spike Milligan from *Silly Verse for Kids*, © Spike Milligan Productions
Ltd. Reprinted by permission

If you can hear (Very quiet) © Barbara Ireson 1984, from *Over and Over Again*,
published by Hutchinson Children's Books. Reprinted by permission.

Noah, Night alarms and **The sea is always moving**, music © Nick Westcott (words
Veronica Clark).

Sir Hector was a spectre from *Not to be taken seriously* by Colin West. © 1984 Colin
West. Reprinted with permission of the author.

The hippo munch © Tamar Swade 1987.

The small ghostie and **Toffee's chewy** by Barbara Ireson from *Rhyme Time 2*, Red
Fox 1984. Reprinted by permission.

The two birds and the Raja © Helen East.

There are big waves by Eleanor Farjeon, © David Higham Associates. Reprinted
by permission.

When we go over to my grandad's © 1979 Michael Rosen from *You Tell Me* by
Roger McGough and Michael Rose (Kestrel 1979) © Michael Rosen 1979. Reprinted
by permission.

**All items marked VC are the copyright of the author, Veronica Clark, © 2002,
1991**

Every effort has been made to trace and acknowledge copyright owners. If any
right has been omitted, the publishers offer their apologies and will rectify this in
subsequent editions following notification.

CONTENTS

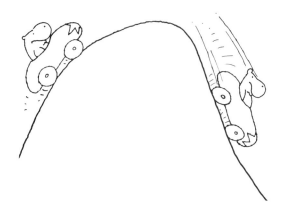

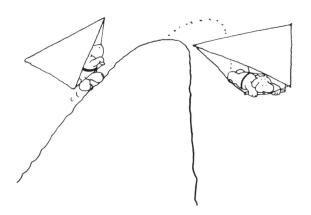

INTRODUCTION

High Low Dolly Pepper approaches teaching music in the classroom through everyday sounds – a way which will be especially welcomed by teachers who do not feel musically confident. In this approach the children's familiar experiences of sound at home and at school are used to explore the basic concepts of music. The teacher can move with the children through a succession of lively and exploratory activities without feeling musically inadequate. *High Low Dolly Pepper* precedes formal music making. It offers a playground of games and exercises which allow young children to investigate all manner of sounds. This is not an approach in which children will be afraid of making mistakes. Their opinion is asked for and valued.

From birth a child is surrounded by a kaleidoscope of sound – voices, weather, body sounds, machinery, animals, vehicles, toys, television, and so on. In *High Low Dolly Pepper* they are asked to recall these sounds, talk about them, analyse them and imitate them. After exploring, the children are invited to use sounds as accompaniments to jingles, poems, songs and stories. They learn to listen analytically, to organise sounds into compositions, and to perform the results.

The structure of the book

The book is divided into five main areas of exploration corresponding to the five basic concepts of music: *timbre*, *volume*, *tempo*, *pitch* and *rhythm* (for an explanation of these terms, please see the glossary on page 96). The five sections are:

> EXPLORING SOUNDS: *timbre*
> LOUDER AND QUIETER: *volume*
> FASTER AND SLOWER: *tempo*
> HIGHER AND LOWER: *pitch*
> LONGER AND SHORTER: *rhythm*

Each section is divided into four units. The units are progressive in the sense that they build on each other. It is therefore advisable to work through the units in the order they are presented. Generally speaking, units one and two of each section are more elementary than units three and four. Teachers wishing to incorporate *High Low Dolly Pepper* into their school music curriculum could consider covering the first two units of each section in the Reception year and Year 1, and the rest in Year 2.

Photocopiable gamesheets

Each unit concludes with a photocopiable gamesheet. This allows the children, singly or in small groups, to practise and consolidate the skills they have learnt in the preceding pages.

Planning your music sessions

Music sessions can last a few moments or half an hour. Ideally young children should have one or more longer music sessions a week plus several short sessions. The structure of this book is designed to make it easy for teachers to plan their music teaching.

Each unit starts with an informal group discussion in which the children are invited to explore their experience of sound and music in relation to the musical concept in question. This introduction is followed by a wide range of follow-up material in which the new idea is developed and practised through poems, jingles, stories, songs and games. Each of these is accompanied by ideas for activities. The activities may take anything from five to fifteen minutes, and are an ideal length for slotting into odd moments.

A teacher planning a longer music session can follow two or three of the activities. He or she should include a mixture of the familiar and the new. Start with something which has previously been practised, then move on to the new material. Conclude with a favourite song or poem or game. Don't be afraid to repeat material. Young children need and enjoy repetition.

Music sessions, especially the short ones, should be informal. Treat them like story times. Let the children sit on the floor. Leave some space at the front for playing instruments or conducting. It is sometimes necessary to sit in a circle, and a few activities require space for movement or dancing.

Signs and signals

It is a good idea to have an easel prepared with large sheets of paper near the area in which the music sessions are conducted. Throughout the book the children are invited to make up written signs and symbols to describe the sounds they are making. You will feel more inclined to try this out if paper and writing materials are readily available.

To conduct your music making, you and the children will have to agree upon a set of signals to start and stop a sound, make it louder or quieter, faster or slower, longer or shorter, higher or lower. A yelled instruction can spoil the effect. Children whose sound production is being controlled by hand gestures will get into the good habit of watching the conductor. Let the children take turns to conduct.

Instruments

It is important to have a selection of good-quality instruments on hand. If you have only a few minutes to spare, it is frustrating to have to waste time sending children off to get instruments. All classrooms should have the following instruments: tambour, tambourine, claves, a woodblock of some kind, two maracas, guiro, jingle bells, a triangle and/or Indian bells. This collection can be supplemented with home-made instruments – shakers, scrapers, coconut shells, claves, and so on. A sound-effects box containing whistles, horns, rattles, squeaky toys, bells and anything else which produces an interesting sound is useful. A pitched instrument such as a xylophone, glockenspiel or set of chime bars will be needed for many activities, and, if not actually a permanent feature of the classroom, should be easily accessible.

Children love to play instruments. Sadly, relatively few young children get the chance to explore their sound potential because they are only brought out on special occasions, and even then only a few children are allowed to play them. It isn't always possible to let every child in the group play an instrument during class music sessions. It is, therefore, important to make instruments available at other times. The children can play the instruments in the music corner (see below). Limit the number of children playing (one to four) and limit the number of instruments available. Make sure the players know the rules concerning handling the instruments and volume of playing (see page 30). In the music corner the children can either try out a prescribed activity as suggested in the book or they can play freely with the instruments. They will often make up music related to things they have tried out in class.

Music corner

Throughout *High Low Dolly Pepper*, suggestions are made for music corner activities. The activities are usually extensions of material covered in the class music sessions. A music corner can be anywhere convenient to teachers and pupils. It can be fixed or moveable, in the classroom, a corridor or a large cupboard, on the floor or on a table. The children should be instructed to play quite quietly. A screen will cut down noise.

Give the children an opportunity to play back to an audience the music they have created.

Recording sounds on cassette

Children can learn a lot about sound and music through listening to their own compositions and accompaniments. It is a good idea to have access to a good quality cassette recorder. One with a built-in microphone and able to run on batteries is both easy and convenient for the children to operate.

Science

Young children are fascinated by the science of sound. In the sections on this the children are taken into areas of scientific exploration which are not so familiar. The rubber bands and the milk bottles are still in evidence, but so are suggestions for measuring volume and pitch, and suggestions for recording findings about voices in relation to body size and mass.

Other areas of the curriculum

High Low Dolly Pepper is cross-curricular in the sense that it touches upon key areas of the infant school curriculum. The activities involve discussion and listening, and the many jingles, poems, songs and stories introduce a wealth of rich vocabulary. Data handling skills are required as the children are invited to find ways of recording their findings. Many of the activities require the children to look closely at the design and function of musical instruments, thus introducing a technological dimension. Throughout, the children are encouraged to express sound in movement, mime, drawing, painting and writing.

Much of the material can be linked to topic work. The thematic index (page 94) will help you to select relevant material.

The scope of *High Low Dolly Pepper* is sufficiently wide and thorough to provide a sound basis for the study of music in the framework of the National Curriculum. Its aim is to make music accessible and fun to pupils and teachers alike. It is hoped that it will encourage teachers to see music as an integral part of the infant school curriculum.

Veronica Clark

1 Body sounds

This unit explores the sounds we can make with our hands and feet, and other parts of the body, and suggests how to utilise these sounds in poems, songs and stories.

HANDS AND FEET

Exploring

Hands – encourage the children to find out how many sounds they can make with their hands (firstly with one hand then with two), e.g.

●Ask them to think of words to describe the sounds, e.g. *tic tic tic* for finger clicks.

Feet – in the same way ask the children to explore the variety of sounds they can make with their feet, with or without shoes, on different floor surfaces. Ask them to make up words to describe them.

Poems with sound

Ask the children to choose hand sounds to accompany the first poem below and foot sounds for the second. Talk about when and where to introduce the sounds, and how to use them, e.g. perhaps as a continuous background sound or just on the words which they describe.

Little wind

Kate Greenaway

Little wind blow on the hill top;
Little wind blow down the plain;
Little wind blow up the sunshine,
Little wind blow off the rain.

Let your feet go tap tap tap

VC

Let your feet go tap tap tap,
Let your heels go snap snap snap.
Then cross your legs and hug your knees –
Be quiet, please.

> **Music corner** – put the poems in the music corner and encourage the children to recite them as they provide the sound effects. Work singly or in pairs.

Storytelling with sound

Talk about sound effects and why they are used. You could play a story tape or an extract you have recorded from a radio show to illustrate sound effects. Ask if the hand sounds they have explored make the children think of other kinds of sounds, e.g. wind, applause, rustling paper, clock ticking.

●Use hands to make sound effects for the first story, and foot sounds for the second. Asterisks indicate the places where sounds might be included.

●Discuss how the sounds you decide on can be used most effectively – should they be loud or quiet, rapid or slow, long or short.

●Think about when it would be appropriate for one child to make the sound, when a small group might be needed, and when all the children can perform.

●Give a clear signal for sounds to begin and end.

Little Red Riding Hood

Little Red Riding Hood walked through the woods picking flowers for her granny. Sometimes she stepped on dry twigs which snapped under her feet *. The breeze rustled the leaves in the tree tops *. Nearby a woodpecker tapped his bill against a tree trunk *. And far away she could hear a wood-cutter chopping down a tree *.

(Continue the story with the children adding their ideas for sounds.)

The frog-welly walk   VC

Barbara was fed up with walking slowly with her mum and little sister so she marched on ahead in her new green frog-wellies *. She came to a huge puddle stretching right across the pavement and she stamped through it * Round the corner lived a dog which barked loudly whenever it heard anyone walk past the gate, so Barbara tiptoed quietly past *. The dog didn't hear her. Barbara scuffed and kicked her way through a pile of crunchy sycamore leaves which had collected near the wall *. Then she stopped and listened. She heard one of her favourite sounds coming along the road towards her. Barbara turned round and ran back to her mum as fast as her frog-wellies would carry her *. 'Mum,' she called, 'please can I have an ice-cream?'

•Repeat a sound from one of the stories and ask the children, with closed eyes, to identify it.

> **Music corner** – let the children make up their own stories requiring hand and, or foot sound effects. They can make a picture of the main events in comic strip fashion. Tell the story to a partner in the music corner. The partner makes the sound effects.
>
>

Copyfeet

One child comes out from the group and makes a sound with his or her feet. The others listen with eyes closed, and try to think of a situation the sound could describe, e.g. running feet – James is being chased by a fierce dog, or irregular tapping – water is dripping onto the floor. Talk about which situations are most appropriate. There is no one correct answer.

Hands can hold and hands can squeeze   VC
(tune: *Oats and beans and barley grow*)

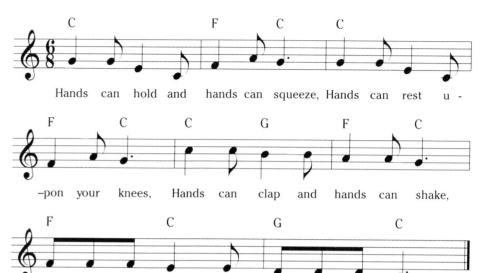

Hands can hold and hands can squeeze, Hands can rest upon your knees, Hands can clap and hands can shake, What kind of sound can (Jo-na-than) make?

•As you sing together, do the actions suggested by the words. Pause at the end of the song. The named child moves behind a screen and makes a hand sound. The other children listen and join in as soon as they have identified it. Sing the song again and name another child.

> **Music corner** – play a game based on the song. The children work in pairs. One child makes a hand sound, the other, with eyes closed, tries to identify it and copy it. If incorrect, the child tries again.

More songs to sing

Add hand and foot sounds to other songs you know. Sing *Here we go round the mulberry bush* to *This is the way we clap our hands*, or *This is the way we walk* (*tiptoe, slide, stamp, shuffle*) *along*. Try *She'll be hopping* (*jumping, stamping*) *round the mountain when she comes*.

MORE BODY SOUNDS

Exploring

Let the children find out how many more sounds they can make with their bodies, e.g. pop finger out of mouth, gently slap bulging cheeks, thump chest, rub hand up and down arm or leg, scratch, slap arm or leg.

If you're feeling blue

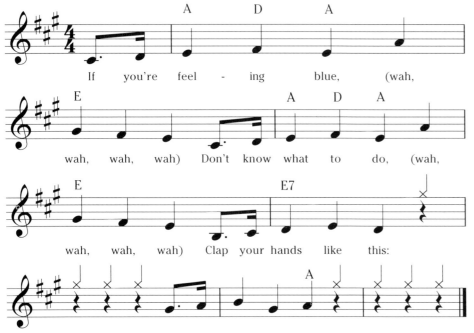

If you're feel - ing blue, (wah,

wah, wah, wah) Don't know what to do, (wah,

wah, wah, wah) Clap your hands like this:

Clap your hands like this:

- Clap hands at the places marked ✗
- Change clap your hands to thump your chest, pop your cheek, knock your knees, stamp your feet etc.
- You can accumulate the sounds: clap your hands like this, thump your chest like this, pop your cheek like this, etc.

Storytelling with sound

Add sound effects to stories. First read the story, then discuss with the children what body sounds could be added. Tell the story again letting the children add the sounds you have agreed on.

IN THE RAINFOREST – *photocopiable gamesheet*

In this game the players are taken on an imaginary trek through a rainforest. They experiment with body sounds – hands, feet, voice, etc, to reproduce the sounds of animals, people and vegetation.

What you need:
- One copy of the gamesheet, coloured and mounted on card if you like.
- Two players
- A die
- Twenty counters in two colours (ten of each)

To play:
Each player places a counter on START. One child shakes the die and moves his or her counter to the appropriate section of the path. If the counter lands on a picture, the players says, 'I went for a walk in the rainforest and I heard . . .' The player then experiments with body sounds until he or she produces a sound to match the picture, e.g. rapid, quiet hand claps for running feet. If the counter lands on an empty space, move on to the next player.

A new counter is used for each go. This means that at the end of the game, when both players have reached FINISH, the players can look back and retrace their journey in sound by making the appropriate sound effects in reverse order.

- The game can be played cumulatively. Each time the players land on a new bit of the path, they repeat the previous sounds they made adding the new one at the end.
- Encourage the players to think about volume, speed and duration of sound, as well as its quality.

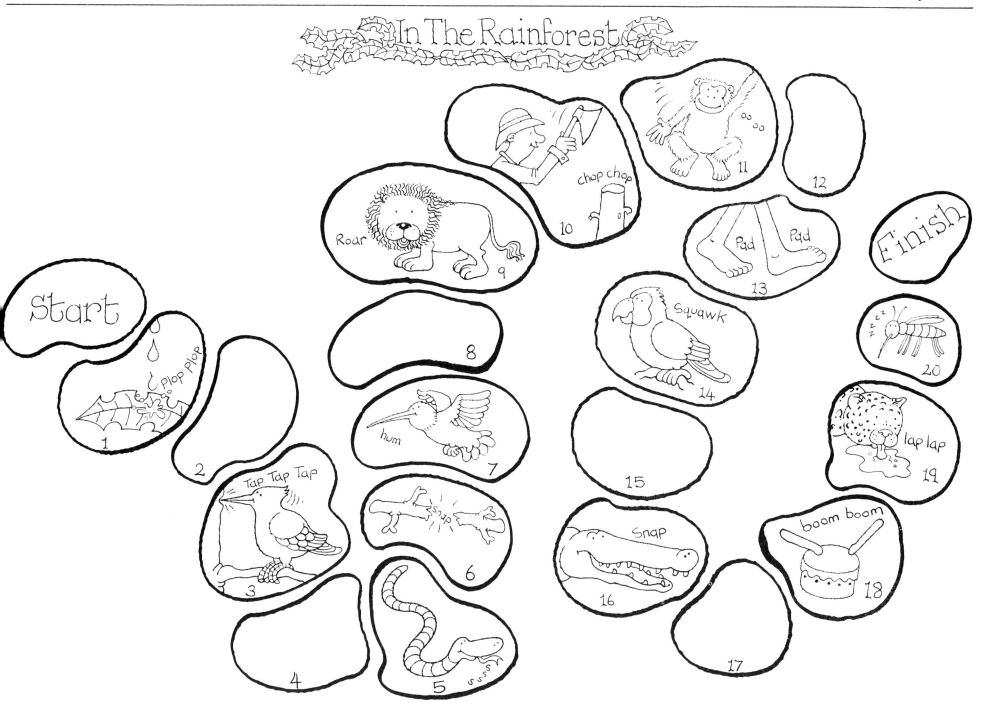

2 Mouth sounds

The mouth and voice are capable of producing a huge range of contrasting and exciting sounds. Children explore these sounds from birth onwards. There are literally hundreds of different sounds which their voices can reproduce in conjunction with mouth shape: huffing and puffing, sneezing, sighing, snoring, panting, whistling, noisy eating, kissing, clicking, humming, etc. They will have explored all kinds of mimicry in their play, pretending to be animals, ghosts, trains, machines, extra-terrestrials, and so on.

Making up accompaniments to poems

The poems which follow provide stimulus for exploring mouth sounds, which in turn can be used to accompany the poems. Read each poem first and ask the children about the sounds it suggests. Let them experiment to find the most appropriate sounds.

● Discuss how the sounds can be shaped into an accompaniment. For instance, in *Granny* they might form a continuous background sound, perhaps starting before the poem to set the scene, and ending after. In *Coughs and sneezes* it may work well to punctuate the poem with sounds at odd moments, whereas in *Toffee's chewy*, you might pause at the places where sounds suggest themselves.

● This type of exercise extends the children's vocabulary. Encourage them to use any new words they find (many of which will be onomatopaeic) in their own poems and stories.

● Try saying words from the poems in appropriate ways – make 'sneeze' sound like a sneeze, slurp the word 'slurp', shout 'hurricane' and whisper 'breeze'.

It's raining, it's pouring

It's raining, it's pouring,
The old man's snoring.
He went to bed and bumped his head
And couldn't get up in the morning.

●Divide into groups – one to chant the poem, one to make snoring sounds, and a third to make rain sounds.

When we go over to my grandad's   *Michael Rosen*

When we go over
to my grandad's
he falls asleep.

While he's asleep
he snores.

When he wakes up,
he says,
'Did I snore?
did I snore?
did I snore?

Everybody says, 'No,
you didn't snore.'

Why do we lie to him?

●Practise slow rhythmic, relaxed breathing and snoring noises.

●Begin with the sleepy breathing sounds, and as the poem progresses, change to snoring. Let the snoring continue for a while before grandad wakes up. Choose one child to say grandad's lines. Everyone else can say 'No you didn't snore.'

Toffee's chewy   *Barbara Ireson*

Toffee's chewy,
Treacle's gooey,
Ice cream's licky,
Honey's sticky,
Nuts are crunchy,
Chocolate's munchy.

All these things I love to eat
But POPCORN is my favourite treat.

●Choose a child or group for each line of the poem. Everyone can chant the last two lines. Follow this with a barrage of popping noises made by popping fingers out of cheeks.
●Add some more food favourites, e.g. *cornflakes are crackly, sherbert's tingly*, etc.

Granny

Spike Milligan

Through every nook and every cranny
The wind blew in on poor old Granny,
Around her knees, into each ear
(And up her nose as well I fear.)

All through the night the wind grew worse,
It nearly made the vicar curse.
The top had fallen off the steeple
Just missing him (and other people).

It blew on man; it blew on beast.
It blew on nun, it blew on priest.
It blew the wig off Auntie Fanny –
But most of all, it blew on Granny.

●*Wind sounds* – try whistling, hissing, and making *sh, fff,* and *ooo* sounds.
●One child or a group reads the poem. Divide the children into three groups. Group one sets the scene with a gentle breeze, and continues through verse one *to the end.* Group two joins in on the second verse and group three on the third. Build up to a hurricane of sound, gradually dying away after the poem ends.

Coughs . . .

It was a cough
That carried him off.
It was a coffin
They carried him off in.

. . . and sneezes

Once a wish,
Twice a letter,
Three times a kiss,
Four times something better.

●Provide a background accompaniment of coughs, sniffles and sneezes for these two jingles.

Night sounds

Thomas Middleton

Midnight's bell goes ting, ting,
  ting, ting,
Then dogs do howl, and not a bird
  does sing
But the nightingale, and she cries
  twit, twit, twit;
Owls then on every bough do sit;
Ravens croak on chimneys' tops;
The cricket in the chamber hops;
The nibbling mouse is not asleep,
But he goes peep, peep, peep, peep, peep;
  And the cats cry mew, mew, mew,
  And still the cats cry mew, mew, mew.

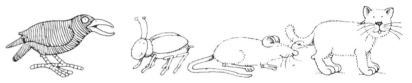

●Use voices as far as possible, but include instruments if the children suggest them.
●When the children know the poem well, replace the sound words (*ting, howl, twit,* etc) with the sound effects.
●Next try making the sound effects on their own in any order or combination to create an impression of night.

> **Music corner** – copy one or two of the shorter poems and display them in the music corner. Encourage the children in pairs, to say the poems aloud and to accompany them with vocal and mouth sound effects.

Guess which sound

After one of the poems, ask a child to go behind a screen and make one of the sounds again (e.g. one of the eating sounds from *Toffee's chewy*). Can the others guess which one it is?

Noah

Words: VC Music: Nick Westcott

Chorus

Well the rain came down And the wa - ters rose, It

swished and it swirled_ round the a - ni - mals' toes.

No - ah said as he o - pened the doors,

'Stand in____ pairs and wipe your paws.'

Verse

1. First came the ducks, *(Quacks)* Followed by the cats, *(Miaows)*

Then came the owls, *(Twit twoo)* Followed by the rats. *(Eeeks)*

2 Then came the sheep . . .
   Followed by the dogs . . .
   Then came the snakes . . .
   Followed by the frogs . . .

3 Then came the pigs . . .
  Followed by the larks . . .
  Then came the ants (*silence*)
  Followed by the sharks . . .

4 Then came the tigers . . .
  Cow and bull . . .
  'STOP!' said Noah, (*clap clap clap*)
  'The ark is full.' (*Hip hip hooray*)

Final chorus
   Well the rain came down and the waters rose,
   It swished and it swirled round Noah's toes.
   Noah said as he closed the doors,
   'I'm glad they came in twos, not fours.'

NOAH SNAP – *photocopiable gamesheet*

This is a snap game for two players.

What you need:
- Two copies of the gamesheet. Mount them on card and cut along the lines so that you have sixteen little cards – eight for each player (the children can colour them in).
- A screen
- An ark (shoe box)

To play:
Each player shuffles their pack of eight cards and places them face down in a pile. The players sit with a screen (e.g. a large book) between them so that they cannot see their partner's cards.

The players turn over their top cards *at the same time,* and make the sound of the animal depicted. They continue until the eight cards have been used up. If they turn over the same animal, they call snap as soon as they recognise each other's sound. The matching pair is put into the 'ark'.

The players shuffle their cards at the end of each round and turn over again. It can take some time for the first few pairs to be matched, but once the ark begins to fill up, the game progresses rapidly. It finishes when all the animals are home and dry.

It's a good idea to limit the game to ten rounds for younger players. At the end of the ten rounds they count up and see how many animals are in the ark.

Noah snap

3 Environmental sounds

Sounds made by objects and materials in the immediate classroom environment can be used to accompany stories, pictures, poems and songs. At the most basic level they can be used to represent what they are (rattling milk bottles to accompany a poem about a milkman), or they can describe something completely different (crumpled tissue paper to make the sound of a fire).

Encourage the children to listen to the sounds they make, to describe them, to experiment with them and to consider what if anything, they remind them of. **Try not to put your ideas into the heads of the children.**

Take care not to dismiss ideas that seem to you to be unsuitable. Always ask for the reasons behind the choices. You may well be surprised by the suitability of the link and by the way in which the children express themselves.

Children sometimes make connections based on movement rather than sound. For example, a child listening to crackly paper being crunched between two hands said that it sounded like bread. His observation was influenced by the kneading movement, not by the sound.

If the children during the course of the school day draw your attention to an interesting sound, try to capitalise on the situation there and then. Can the sound be made quietly? Gradually get louder. Longer or shorter? Higher or lower sounding? Do they like the sound? Can they draw it? Hunt around for a poem or story into which the sound could be incorporated.

Exploring sound sources

A classroom is an Aladdin's cave of sound. Here are just some areas you might explore:

– **milk crate:** try rattling a crate of full or empty bottles, tap two bottles together, listen to the quiet sound of moving air as the foil lid is pressed in, make a recording of milk being drunk, blow across the top of an empty bottle, rustle clean foil tops together.

– **counting and writing equipment:** tap and twang rulers, rattle pencils and crayons, listen to the sound of cutting scissors.

– **paper and card:** listen to flapping, ripping, crumpling, flicking and folding paper.

– **art and craft materials:** shake and tap buttons, corks, nails, pasta.

– **objects on the nature table:** rattle seed pods, crumple leaves, shake shells and stones, snap and rub twigs.

– **outdoor sounds:** listen from inside the classroom to the sounds outside. Can the children identify them?

Collecting sound groups

Another way to develop the children's sound awareness is to listen for a specific type of sound:

● For example, let them try to find as many different snapping sounds as they can – poppers, purse fasteners, wooden bricks banged together, popping plastic air bubbles in packaging, ruler flicked against hard surface, fitting parts of construction toys together, elastic bands held taut and twanged against a hard surface, snapping or crumpling plastic pots. If they suggest finger snaps, or tongue clicks, which are body sounds, let these be included.

● Here are some more ideas for collections: clicking, tapping, crashing, blowing, rattling, scraping, jangling, swishing.

● The sounds you find can be used in storytelling, poetry, songs and with pictures. For example, you could use the snapping sounds as a background to the song *London's burning*, or a poem about fireworks, or a story about crocodiles.

Making up accompaniments to poems

There are many poems and jingles which lend themselves to this kind of accompaniment. Below is a short collection. As before (see Mouth sounds) read the poem then discuss with the children how and when to make the sounds. Some ideas are given, but ignore them if the children have plenty of their own.

After a while you might find that you have quite a collection of useful sound-makers. These can be kept in a box, handy for the children to choose from at storytime or when reading poetry.

Hot pants

The boy stood on the burning deck,
His feet were full of blisters;
The flames came up and burned his pants,
And now he wears his sister's.

● Try crackly paper and snapping twigs.

Beech leaves

James Reeves

In Autumn down the beechwood path
The leaves lie thick upon the ground.
It's there I love to kick my way
And hear the crisp and crashing sound.

I am a giant, and my steps
Echo and thunder to the sky.
How the small creatures of the woods
Must quake and cower as I go by.

●Try shaking or scrumpling newspaper for dry leaves, or – 'walk' hands through a deep box full of the real thing.

●Think of quiet scurrying and scratching sounds to depict the frightened woodland creatures running to hide.

There are big waves

Eleanor Farjeon

There are big waves and little waves,
    Green waves and blue,
Waves you can jump over,
    Waves you dive through,
Waves that rise up
    Like a great water wall,
Waves that swell softly
    And don't break at all.
Waves that can whisper,
    Waves that can roar,
And tiny waves that run at you
    Running on the shore.

●Use a selection of boxes with a different filler in each, e.g. beads, rice, buttons, Lego, sand. Gently roll or tip the boxes from end to end. Try to get a range of volume to match the words of the poem.

●Experiment with paper – ripped and crumpled – to make more wave or sea sounds. Can you make the sound of moving shingle using pebbles or gravel?

Sampan

Tao Lang Pee

Waves lap lap
Fish fins clap clap
Brown sails flap flap
Chop-sticks tap tap.

Up and down the long green river,
Oh hey, oh hey, lanterns quiver,
Willow branches brush the river,
Oh hey, oh hey, lanterns quiver.

Chop-sticks tap tap
Brown sails flap flap
Fish fins clap clap
Waves lap lap.

●You might try bringing in the sounds quietly one by one as they are mentioned, continuing through the middle stanza, and dropping them one by one in the final stanza.

Sir Hector

Colin West

Sir Hector was a spectre
And he loved a lady ghost;
At midnight he'd collect her
And he'd drive her to the coast.

And there upon the shingle
They would rattle all their bones,
And ocean sounds would mingle
With their melancholy moans.

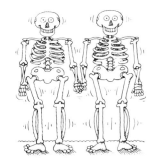

●Try rattling Lego or pencils for rattling bones, moan through cardboard tubes and slide rice grains around a shoe box for water on shingle. Add a few seagulls.

Music corner – put one or two of the poems (or extracts from them) in the music corner with a collection of sound effect materials. Ask the children, singly or in pairs, to provide an accompaniment to the words.

How did you know it was me?   *VC*

First read the story without sounds.

• Talk about the sounds in the story. How did Jenny know who was coming towards her? What was special about each sound?

• Ask the children to copy the sounds using voices, bodies and the sound makers you have been exploring in this unit. Experiment and discuss to find the best effects.

• Practise starting each sound off quietly then slowly increase the volume. Stop the sound at the loudest point.

• Decide upon a starting and stopping signal.

• Read the story again incorporating the sounds into the text where they are mentioned. You will need to practise a few times to achieve satisfactory results.

Jenny's house was right at the end of one of those roads which don't go any further. The road ended just by Jenny's gate. Roads like this are called cul-de-sacs or dead ends.

Jenny had made a den in her garden. She had propped an old door against the wall by the front gate and filled in the gaps with an old blanket and a piece of plastic sheeting. You couldn't see the den from the road, and you couldn't see the road from the den, but when Jenny was tucked away inside her pretend house she could hear the traffic. Sometimes the cars stopped before they reached her house, sometimes the cars drove to the end of the road and turned round by Jenny's gate before going back to the main road, and sometimes, (but not very often), the cars drove right up the road and stopped. Then Jenny knew she had visitors.

One Friday morning right at the beginning of the summer holiday, Jenny was sitting in her den looking at a comic and waiting for her friend Sam. She was trying to do one of those puzzles where you have to look for hidden objects, and Jenny had just found the sixth umbrella when she heard footsteps coming along the pavement towards her. They got louder and louder. She knew it wasn't Sam – Sam wore trainers. Whoever this was wore clicky shoes. Who could it be? 'I know,' she thought, 'It's mum's friend, Shirley.'

'Hello, Shirley,' she called.

'Hello, Jenny, wherever you are,' said Shirley as she came in through the gate. 'How did you know it was me?' Jenny laughed.

Jenny was in the middle of a story about Bonzo the mischievous puppy when she heard a car approaching. It was noisy and rattly. 'Visitors,' thought Jenny, 'But who can it be? I know,' she thought, 'It's Uncle John, he's got an old banger which always sounds as though it's about to break down.'

'Hello, Uncle John,' she shouted, as Uncle John got out of the car.

'Hello, Jenny, wherever you are,' said Uncle John. 'But how did you know it was me?' Jenny smiled.

Jenny almost missed her next visitor. She heard a quiet scratching noise coming towards her then a snuffling and a sniffing.

'Hello, Rufus,' she called. 'Come here, good dog.'

Rufus padded over to the den, sniffed around, barked, wagged his tail and disappeared up the garden path.

Jenny was on page five of her comic helping a rabbit through a maze to its carrot when she heard a jingle-jangle sound getting nearer and nearer. It stopped just outside the gate.

'Three pints please,' called Jenny from her hiding place.

'Hello, Jenny – wherever you are,' said the milkman, sounding puzzled. 'But how did you know it was me?' Jenny smiled.

Jenny was on the last page of her comic and wishing Sam would hurry up and arrive when she heard a rolling, rumbling sound. It got nearer and nearer. The sound stopped suddenly with a scrunch and Jenny heard something being pushed into the letter box on the gate.

'Hello, Damien,' shouted Jenny. 'You're late.'

'Hello,' shouted Damien, 'I overslept.'

Jenny finished her comic. She rolled it up like a telescope, pushed it through a crack in the sheeting and looked up into the trees. She saw a blackbird with a worm in its mouth. It flew off towards next door's garden and Jenny tried to keep it in view through her telescope. Suddenly there was a very loud 'BOO' from just outside the den.

'Sam,' said Jenny, 'you made me jump. Anyway, how did you know where I was?' Sam smiled.

Just a load of rubbish

VC

Feel a - round in my big box,

Take your time...

(Pause for as long as you need)

What have you got?

Chorus

Just a load of rub - bish but it makes a love - ly sound.

Shake it high, shake it low, Shake it all a - round.

This is a game-song. To play it you need a collection of junk instruments. Let the children construct and select them. The collection could include various pots (with secure lids) partially filled with beads, pasta, buttons, sand, etc to make shakers; stout cardboard boxes and tins for drums with a selection of sticks and brushes for beaters; corrugated card stuck firmly onto wooden bricks or fig boxes for scrapers; rolled-up newspaper cut into strips down one end to make a paper shaker, and so on.

To play:
You will need a large cardboard box with an open end. Put a selection of your junk instruments into the box, and as you sing the verse, let one of the children, with eyes closed, feel around inside and select an instrument to play in the chorus in the way the words direct.

●Change *shake* to *tap, scrape, rattle,* etc. Change *high/low* to *quietly/loudly, long/short, fast/slow.*

●When the children are familiar with the game and with the sounds made by the junk instruments, the selection and playing can take place behind a screen and the listening children can guess what is being played.

JUST JUNK – *photocopiable gamesheet*

This is a game for four players and a leader. The four players have one strip of four boxes each. They use the strips to record the 'junk' sounds made by the leader. Before playing, let the children try out the sounds which the junk instruments make.

What you need:
●One copy of the gamesheet, cut into four strips.

●Six items of junk. Number them 1–6.

●A screen.

To play:
The leader takes the junk instruments behind the screen. He or she writes four numbers from 1 to 6 in the table provided. They can be in any order and one or more may be repeated, e.g. 1 5 5 6.

The leader plays the junk items one by one in the order of the numbers selected. The listening children write the numbers of the junk items in the boxes provided and in the order they hear them played. They can refer to the picture of the instruments on the gamesheet.

When the four numbers have been played and recorded, the screen is removed and the leader repeats the sound sequence, and the listeners check their results. Play again with a different leader.

Let the children make up their own gamesheets, select their own six junk instruments and number them.

Just junk

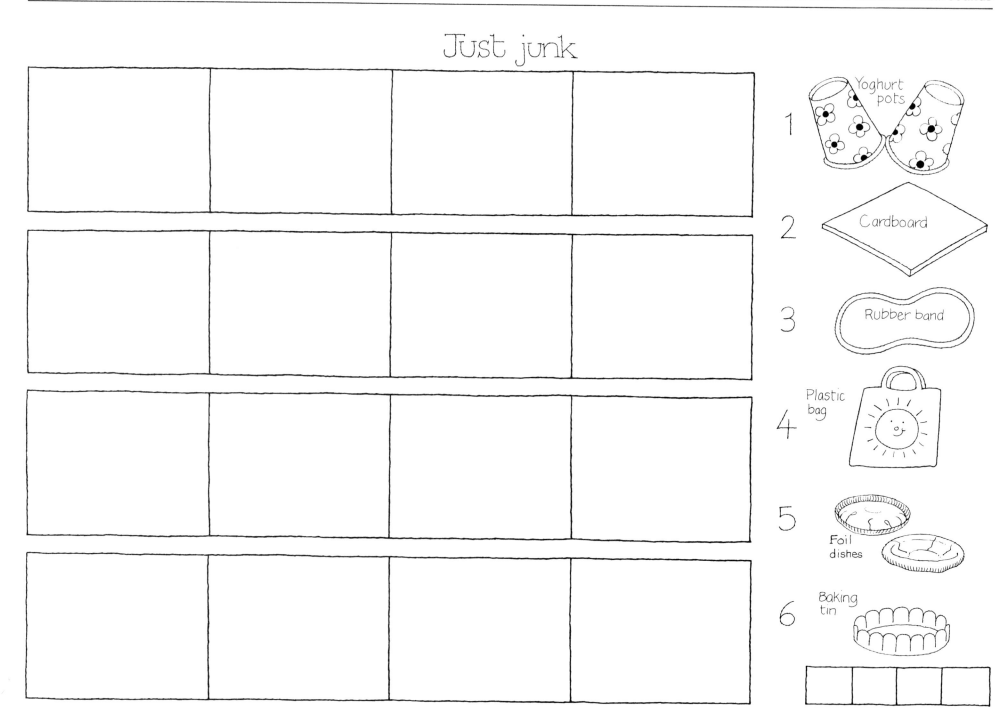

1 Yoghurt pots

2 Cardboard

3 Rubber band

4 Plastic bag

5 Foil dishes

6 Baking tin

4 Instrumental sounds

In this unit, seasons and festivals provide the stimulus for sound exploration with classroom instruments (see the introduction for a check list of those you should have). Ideas for using the instruments are provided, but before referring to them, ask for the children's own ideas.

Let them use another sound source (body, mouth or environmental) if they don't think the instrumental sound is satisfactory (their experience in the previous three units should be helpful here). They may need several sessions on each of the themes to develop their ideas fully.

Using posters – for each of the themes try to find a suitable poster-sized picture to show the children. Discuss what sounds are represented in the picture – are they loud or quiet or in-between? Are they regular or 'now and then' sounds? Are they high-pitched or low-pitched or in-between. Display the poster in the music corner so that the children can experiment individually with sounds to match those they see in the picture.

Using movement – the themes can be linked with movement and drama, accompanied by the instrumental sounds the children devise, e.g.

Autumn – drift and fall like leaves and seeds, stamp on dry leaves then brush them up with generous sweeping movements. Leap and flick outwards in imitation of flames and sparks, sinking into a small mound of ash to finish.

Chinese New Year – individually or in a line of three or more children, wind round the room, in a dragon dance. Skip, march, leap or creep, each child copying the leader at the head of the dragon.

Spring – slowly rise from the ground like a shoot, swell like a bud. Send out roots and leaves. Wriggle like tadpoles, gambol like lambs, dart around like young chicks.

Summer – mime various beach activities – exploring rock pools, throwing pebbles, digging sand castles and paddling. Pretend to be the advancing tide. Form a line and slowly creep across the floor, advancing and retreating like waves until high tide is reached. Half the group can play on the beach while the rest mime the tide.

AUTUMN

Ask the children to list the things which remind them of autumn, and encourage them to experiment with instruments to describe the scenes they suggest. Try working in groups, taking one scene each. Here are some possibilities:

Wind – rub hands or brush over a large surface such as a cymbal or the skin of a large drum or tambour. Discuss how these and other instrumental effects compare with the wind sounds the children made in previous units. Can they use volume variations to suggest sudden gusts of wind?

Falling seeds, fruit and leaves – talk about the different ways these fall to the ground: drifting, twirling, thudding, according to shape, size, weight, and so on. How can the children describe this with instruments? Experiment with pitched percussion using different playing techniques, e.g. rub and tap the bars and use different kinds of beater. Try skinned instruments for more decisive, thudding sounds.

Walking on dry leaves – find a way of making the evenly-spaced, crunching sounds of walking through dry leaves – a good contrast to the randomly spaced sounds above.

Sweeping up dead leaves – discuss how the sounds differ according to the surface being swept – earth, pavement, rough tarmac, gravel. Can they find an instrumental sound for each? (Guiros, sandpaper, corrugated paper, card, a drum skin, and a selection of brushes would be useful.)

Bonfires – ask the children for words to describe the sounds of a bonfire (e.g. roaring, spitting, hissing, crackling, etc). How can they describe them instrumentally?

• When the children are satisfied with the sounds they have devised, help them to create a sound sequence of autumnal scenes based on the ideas above, e.g.

first the wind is heard blowing gently, then more fiercely through the trees in the park – seeds, nuts, apples, leaves tumble to the ground – the park keeper arrives, scrunching through the dried leaves – he sweeps them into a pile and burns them.

• Discuss how and whether to overlap the sounds and whether any sounds need to be continuous.

WINTER

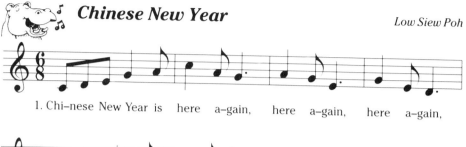

Chinese New Year

Low Siew Poh

1. Chi-nese New Year is here a-gain, here a-gain, here a-gain,

Chi-nese New Year is here a-gain, let us all re-joice.——

2 Look at the dragon breathing flames,
   breathing flames, breathing flames,
   Look at the dragon breathing flames,
   roar, roar, roar.

3 Dragon is leaping with the drum ...
   leap, leap, leap.

4 Crackers are banging in the street ...
   crack, crack, crack.

5 Children have packets of money to spend ...
   clink, clink, clink.

6 Everyone dances through the streets ...
   let us all rejoice.

●After singing the song together discuss with the children how they can devise a piece of music to describe a dancing dragon or lion.

●Talk about how the dragon moves (marching, running, leaping, skipping, shuffling, sidestepping, weaving, pouncing, pausing, and so on).

●How can they describe instrumentally its dancing steps, roars, snarls, flames, snapping teeth, lashing tail and head, and also perhaps the sounds of the accompanying drums and cymbals, jingling money packets, and exploding fire crackers.

SPRING

Discuss spring weather, plants, animals, colours, growth changes, activities, and so on.

Talk about things which could be described instrumentally, e.g.

A hatching chick – tapping within the egg as the baby bird struggles to get out, cracking shell, peeping of the chick, its darting run.

Tadpoles – shivering frogspawn, wriggling tails, moving water

Lambs – wobbly first steps, springing run, high-pitched bleat

Rain showers – sudden downpours falling on leaves, grass, pavements, followed by bright sunshine

A hedgehog waking from hibernation – rustles, stretches, yawns, slow movements followed by faster ones

Colours – the children might try to make an impression in sound of quite abstract concepts such as shape or colour, e.g. that of different coloured flowers – a yellow daffodil, clusters of pink and white blossom, deep blue and purple hyacinths, a slender orange crocus. Can they make their flowers grow from first shoot to fully open flower? Allow them complete freedom in their choice of sounds.

Music corner – draw pictures or find photographs of some of the things you have discussed – chicks, rain showers, flowers, etc, and put them in the music corner along with a selection of instruments. Let the children experiment individually or in pairs.

●Try building a description of winter turning to spring through a sequence of sounds the children have devised. Here is one idea for organising it: after selecting and experimenting with sounds to represent the cold of winter, and the warmth of spring, arrange the children in a large semi-circle with the cold sounds in one half and the warm sounds in the other. Conduct by moving your hand round the semi-circle starting at the cold end. Let a child conduct.

SUMMER

This song about the sea will allow the children to provide a continuous sound of moving water first calm, then rough. Some suggestions for instruments are given but use the children's own ideas if you can.

The sea is always moving

Words: VC
Music: Nick Westcott

1. The sea is al-ways moving, e - ven when it's calm. It

laps the shore and strokes our toes. It's kind. It's warm.

2 The sea is always moving;
   When the tempest blows
   It beats the shore and roars and foams,
   It's cruel. It's cold.

●Let the children experiment with instruments – standard and improvised – to describe the following aspects of a calm sea:

lapping waves – quiet maracas, tambourines shaken gently, rice or sand tipped slowly from side to side in a shoe box.

breeze – quiet roll on cymbal, vocal sounds

sparkling waves – jingles, triangles, indian bells, glocks

sunshine – gong, two or three chimes or metallophone bars struck together to produce a warm, resonant sound

●Now can the children create an effect of:

crashing waves – tambourines, cymbals, noisy shakers

foam – jingles

tempest – loud rolls on the cymbal

surging waves – rub bars of xylophone rapidly with beater, first loudly then quietly; repeat the pattern

grinding pebbles – put stones in a box and roll them around

Signs and signals

Make a frieze, one half depicting the 'kind' sea, the other, the 'cruel' sea. Use a pointer to indicate which individual sounds are to be played or move the pointer across from left to right to indicate a change from storm to a warm, calm day on the beach.

FIREWORK NIGHT – *photocopiable gamesheet*

This is a game for two children. Before playing it, talk with the children about firework sounds: some fizz, some screech like a siren or whistle, some crackle, pop or explode.

Imitate the sounds with voices and other body sounds. Try using instruments. Cheap plastic party toys – whistles, sirens, rattles and blowers – would be useful here. Think about whether the sounds would be long or short, fast or slow, loud or quiet.

What you need:
●One copy of the gamesheet mounted on card. (Ask the children to cut out the six firework pictures and colour them in. Make sure they are familiar with their names and the kinds of sounds they make.)
●A selection of sound-makers – conventional and improvised.

To play:
Shuffle the cards and put them in a pile face downwards. The two players take it in turns to turn over the top card and make the sound of the firework displayed.

●Vary the game by dividing the cards into two piles of three – one set per player. The players turn over their top cards together and make the appropriate firework sounds *at the same time.*

Firework night

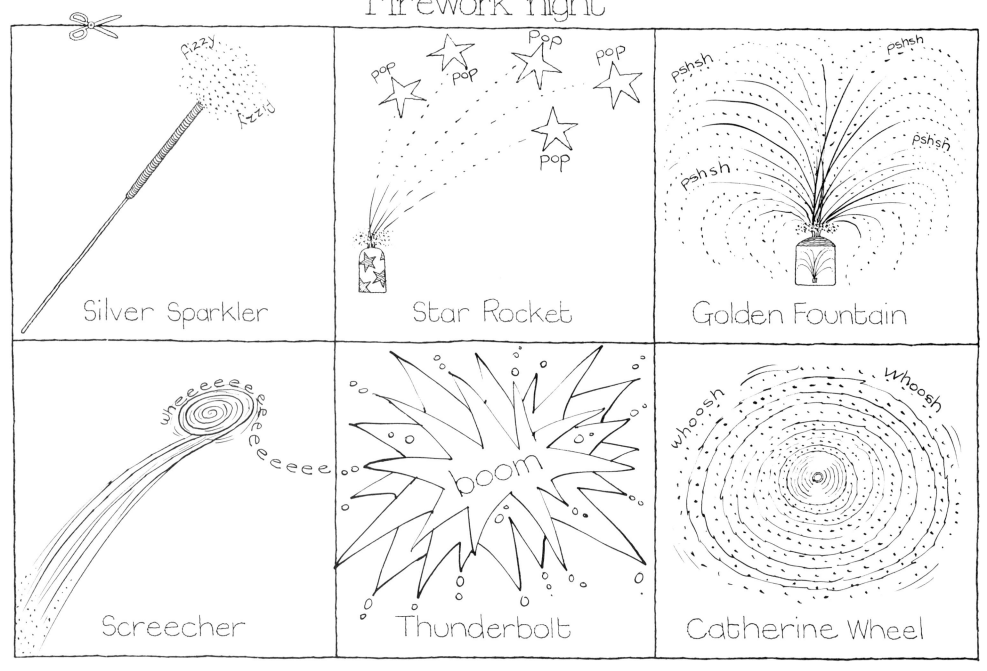

The science of sound – *exploring sounds*

Movement

Sound is caused by movement:

●Ask the children to sit quite still on the floor for a few moments and to listen to each other. What do they notice? Can they keep so still that no body sounds at all can be heard?

●Now ask half the group to go and sit on chairs. The stationary children should listen to the moving children and identify the various body and other sounds which they hear. Swap over.

Vibrations

The waves which travel to our ears and are translated into sound, are produced by vibrations.

●Stretch a rubber band between the fingers or across a large plastic margarine tub, and pluck it.

●Put the end of a ruler on the edge of a table with the rest of it sticking over the edge. Hold the part which is on the table firmly in place and twang the protruding end.

●Sprinkle chalk dust or talcum powder on the upper surface of a large suspended cymbal and gently tap the rim. Watch the chalk dance.

●Put a few grains of rice on the skin of a large drum or tambour and gently tap the surface. Why does the rice bounce up and down?

●Pluck the strings of a guitar. Do all the strings vibrate at the same speed?

Ask the children to draw pictures of these experiments and write about them.

Vibrations and musical instruments

Let the children play some of your school percussion instruments and decide what is vibrating to produce a sound.

●Which sounds could be heard longest? Which were the shortest? Why?

Catching sound waves

In order for a sound to be heard its sound waves have to be caught by our ears. Try 'catching' a sound in different ways. Tap a tambourine several times (try to use the same amount of force each time) and each time ask the children to listen in a different way:

– facing the sound source
– facing away from the sound source
– with ears covered
– with ears cupped

●Which method helped the children to hear the sound best? Which was least effective?

●Look at the ears of different types of animals. What do the children notice about them? Which animals have very big ears? Which have small ears? Why? What can some animals do to hear a sound better?

What can sound waves travel through?

Set up some simple experiments to help the children listen to sounds travelling through water, metal, wood, the earth, plastic, cloth, air and so on. For example:

Water – fill a balloon with water. Hold a ticking watch or kitchen timer against the side of the balloon. Ask a child to press one ear against the other side of the balloon. Cover the other ear. Can the ticks be heard? How clearly can they be heard?

Wood – put the same watch on a wooden table or bench and ask a child to listen with one ear pressed against the wood. Cover the other ear. Try moving the watch or timer further along the bench – how far does the sound travel? How far does the sound travel through the air?

Metal – try the same experiment using a metal radiator. Try tapping a message. How far does the message travel along the pipes and radiators? How far away can the same tapped message be heard through the air?

Air – hold a short cardboard tube to your mouth with one hand and sing an extended *ah* or *oo*. While singing, cover the open end with your hand. Why does covering the open end of the tube stop the sound? Remind the children that in this experiment the sounds waves are movements of air. If the air is prevented from moving, there can be no sound. The same principle applies when children make a war cry by moving the hands on and off the mouth.

1 Quiet sounds

This unit aims to help the children become more aware of quiet times in their daily lives, and to explore quietness in music making.

You can make quietness in class more fun through games. Instead of shouting for attention, ring a small bell quietly. Tell the children you are going to close your eyes while they line up, sit on the carpet, put their pencils away, etc. Can they do it so quietly that you can't hear them moving? Some young children welcome a quiet working environment and feel more secure in it.

Exploring

- When and why is it necessary to be very quiet e.g. in hospital, at church, at school, at home.
- Talk about sounds that are very quiet:
  - some weather sounds (light rain on grass, a breeze)
  - some animals (a cat stalking a bird, a snake, mice)
  - some home sounds (electric clock, newspaper rustling)
  - some school sounds (pencils on paper, scissors cutting)
  - sounds which are quiet because they are a long way off.

Magic spell

Tell the children you are going to cast a magic spell over them which will make them quiet and still. As long as the spell lasts they should listen to all the sounds around and try to remember them. Keep your hands (or wand) extended for about a minute. Afterwards talk about the sounds – were they near or far, made by people or machines? etc.

Signs and signals

- Introduce the musical sign *p*, meaning play or sing quietly (from the Italian *piano*, meaning quiet). Make a large lollipop sign with the letter *p* written boldly on one side. (Keep the other side for the *f* symbol meaning loud.) Display the *p* sign during quiet activities.
- Decide together on a hand sign meaning play or sing quietly, e.g. hands held palms together or finger to lips.

Body sounds

Copy me quietly

Let the children take turns to demonstrate a quiet body sound they can make, e.g. stroking sleeve, tapping fingernails together. Choose a child to initiate a series of very quiet body sounds. The rest of the children copy. Try making two or more quiet sounds at the same time, or in sequence.

Sergeant Silent says

Stand to attention and mouth a series of instructions to your children, e.g. stand up, rub your nose, turn around, stand up straight. The instructions should be obeyed quietly.

Singing together

Sing some of your favourite action songs, e.g. *John Brown's Baby*, *Heads, shoulders, knees and toes*. Leave out an action word each time and just make the action sound. Keep going until you have a whole sequence of quiet body sounds.

Vocal sounds

Ask the children to experiment to find quiet vocal sounds, e.g.

fffff   a sigh   hissssss   shhhh

Night night

Night night, sleep tight,
Mind the bugs don't bite tonight.
If they do, hug them tight,
They won't come back another night.

- Chant this jingle quietly together.
- When the children know it well, mouth the words – shape them with the mouth, letting only a tiny amount of sound escape.
- Divide into two groups – one to mouth the poem, the other to make an accompaniment of quiet bug-biting noises, e.g. by softly clicking teeth together.

Mice at home

Ask the children in pairs to create a sound picture of mouse family life – when the cat's about. It can be as fanciful as they like. Let the children take turns to play their mouse music using vocal or body sounds, and instruments as well if they wish. The others listen then say what they think the mice were doing. Here are some ideas:

nibbling crumbs

making a pot of lavender tea

playing 'snap'.

● Ask the children to write on small cards some words or phrases the mice might use when rocking their babies to sleep. Display them as a mobile or on a board in the music corner. Encourage the children to whisper them in odd moments.

Instrumental sounds

p p p

Select about ten different instruments and place them quietly on the floor in front of the same number of children. Ask one child to pick up his or her instrument and make a quiet sound with it. As soon as the sound stops the next child picks up his or her instrument and plays.

● Discuss how the quiet sounds were produced. Were some instruments easier to play quietly than others? Why?

● How many different quiet sounds could the children find on each instrument?

Woodland warnings

Divide the children into four groups. Give each the name of a woodland animal, e.g. woodmice, squirrels, foxes, badgers, owls, hedgehogs etc. Practise moving like the animals. Choose an instrumental sound for each creature. To play the game ask everyone to move quietly through a pretend wood. On hearing their sound, the animals in that group freeze. They stay still until the sound stops. The other animals keep moving. You can freeze two or more groups at once.

Chinese whispers

Stand about eight children in a row. Give each an instrument. Play a short pattern of quiet sounds to the first child. This child listens carefully, turns to the second child and repeats the pattern as accurately as possible. Keep it *quiet*. When the message gets to the end of the line, compare the final sound with the first sound and decide how accurately it has been passed on.

Music corner – put a few instruments in the music corner next to a sleeping doll or teddy. Invite the children to:

Make up sleepy music for Ted

Environmental sounds

If you can hear   *Barbara Ireson*

If you can hear
A spoon stirring,
A clock ticking,
A mouse scratching,
A cat purring,
Then it's very very very very
    very quiet

● Make up an accompaniment to the poem using classroom or homemade instruments, voices and body sounds.
● Choose four children – one for each sound – to go behind a screen and make the sounds one at a time. Can the others guess which is which? Try two or more sounds together.

Night alarms

Words: VC Music: Nick Westcott

Me - lo - dy was snug-gled down in bed one night, Her

dad had been and gi - ven her a kiss. She was

just a - bout to close her eyes and go to sleep, When she

heard a lit - tle noise like this– *(Pause for sound effects)*

'Dad, dad, there's some-thing in my room, It's

giv - ing me an aw – ful fright.' 'It was

on - ly the *ham-ster in its wheel,* my dear, Close your

eyes and go to sleep, good - night.'

Many young children are frightened by night-time sounds and this song might help them to come to terms with their worries.

● Talk about the sounds that they hear as they are lying in bed, for instance water in the pipes, voices through walls, the wind, pet hamster in its wheel, cats in the street, passing cars, a door banging, floor creaking, someone shouting outside. What sort of things do the children *imagine* these sounds to be?

● Sing the song together and let the children take turns to make a sound after 'a little noise like this ...' and then sing what it really was after 'it was only ...' e.g. 'it was only the water in the pipes, my dear.' They can use their voices, bodies, home-made or classroom instruments to reproduce the sounds.

Here are suggestions for sounds they might hear: *It was only the water in the pipes/slamming of a door/rumble of a train.*

CREEPY CASTLE *– photocopiable gamesheet*

This is a game for two people. One of them wanders round the ruined castle and is frightened by the mysterious sounds produced by creaking doors, rattling chains, and so on. The other player provides the quiet sound effects.

What you need:
● One copy of the gamesheet
● A counter or small figure to represent the exploring child

To play:
The explorer places the counter on any one of the faces. The partner provides a suitable, quiet sound effect. The explorer draws a picture in the thought bubble of what he or she *fears* might be the cause of the sound in a creepy castle, e.g. the hoot-ing owl might be a ghost. When all the sounds have been explored, take a new gamesheet and swap over. At the end, the children can compare the spooky 'answers' they came up with. There is space on the sheet for the children to draw in a few ideas of their own.

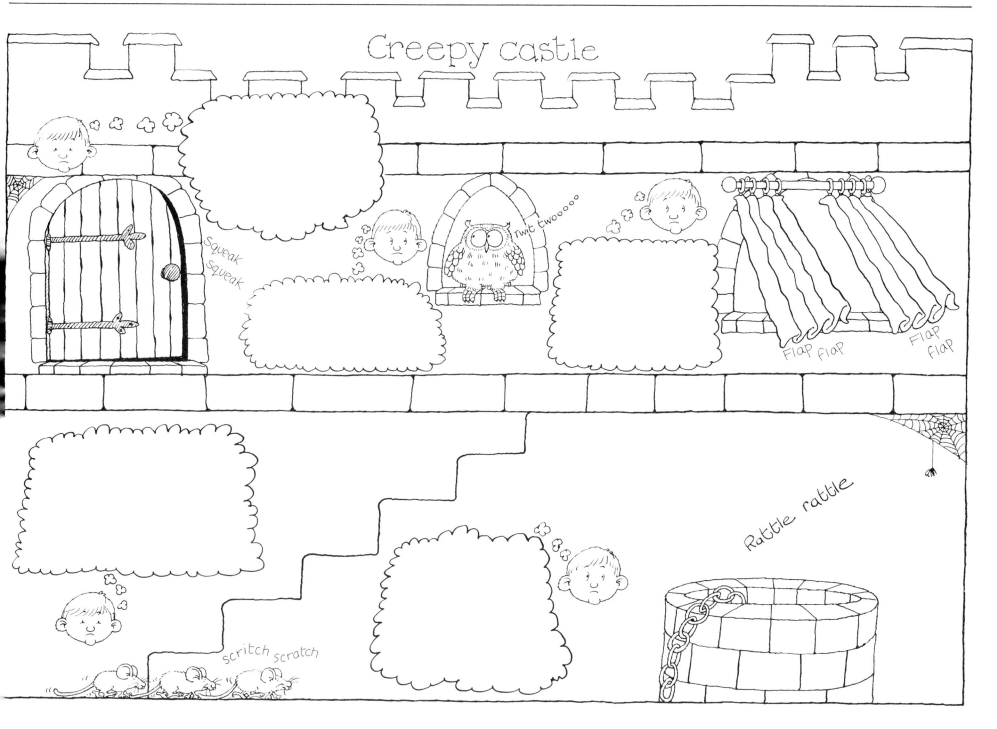

2 Loud sounds

When several children are gathered together they will generate noise! Here the children are encouraged to differentiate between noisy and loud sounds. They imitate them with voices and instruments and, it is hoped, learn when loud sounds are effective and necessary and when they are to be avoided.

Exploring

- Talk about loud sounds:
– babies crying, people quarrelling, telephone bells, loud music, engines, cheering crowds, playground noise, balloons popping, police and ambulance sirens.

- Why are each of these sounds loud?

- Which involve just one person or thing, and which involve several?

- Conduct a survey to see which of these loud sounds are liked and which are not liked.

Signs and signals

- Introduce the musical sign *f* meaning play or sing loudly (from the Italian *forte*, meaning loud). Draw the *f* sign on the other side of your volume lollipop (see page 24). Display the *f* side during loud music activities.

- Decide with the children on a hand signal which will mean play or sing loudly, e.g. hands spread wide apart.

f   *p*

Vocal sounds

- Find a convenient place to let each child shout his or her own name as loudly as possible. Can they *say* their names loudly without shouting?

- Talk about occasions when it is necessary or understandable to shout, e.g. when giving a warning, when in pain, or when you want someone far off to hear you.

- What words are used in these situations? Make a table like the example below, then let the children take turns to say the words loudly.

- Can they match the expression of their voices to the meaning of the words, e.g. sound angry for 'BAD DOG' or urgent for 'WATCH OUT!'

warnings –	STOP	DANGER	watch out
attention seeking –	hello	mum	HELP
in pain –	ow!	aaaaaah	
in excitement –	hooray	come on the blues	
in anger –	stop it!	let go	BAD DOG

Billy is blowing his trumpet

Billy is blowing his trumpet,
Bert is banging a tin,
Betty is crying for mummy,
And Bob has pricked Ben with a pin. (Ouch!)
Baby is crying out loudly;
He's out on the lawn in his pram.
I am the only one quiet
'Cause I've got my mouth full of jam!

- Choose a child to make each sound and let them practise making it into a continuous sound.

- Read the poem and let the children join in with their sounds as each is mentioned. You should have a fairly noisy accumulation by the end of the poem. Stop abruptly on 'jam' and listen to the silence.

Watch out!

VC

2 'Turn around, Mrs Bird.'
'There's nothing after me.'
'Yes there is, Mrs Bird.'
'I'm safe as safe can be.'
'No you're not, Mrs Bird,
Don't pretend you haven't heard,
Master Cat is right behind you, Mrs Bird.'

3 'Turn around, Master Cat.'
'There's nothing after me.'
'Yes there is, Master Cat.'
'I'm safe as safe can be.'
No you're not, Master Cat,
(CLAP CLAP CLAP)
It's me right behind you,
Now SCAT!'

• Discuss with the children where in the song to sing loudly and urgently, and where to sing softly.

• Add body and instrumental sounds to words such as 'SCAT' and 'snapping at your tail'.

• Choose individual children to be the worm, the bird, and the cat. They take it in turns to sing the words in italic. If preferred these words can be spoken, rather than sung.

More songs to sing

Look at other songs you know which contain words or phrases that can be sung or accompanied loudly. (Make sure the children can hear and feel the difference in their voices between shouting and singing loudly.) Try these: *Ten fat sausages, If you're happy and you know it, Hill and gully.*

Instrumental sounds

Careful please!

No musical instrument should be played so loudly that there is a danger of it being spoilt. Neither should the instruments be played so loudly that the sound is distorted. Experiment with playing the instruments loudly and talk about each instrumental type. It is possible to produce an exciting range of volume on a large cymbal, whereas there isn't much difference between loud and quiet maraca shakes. Are some instruments more difficult to play loudly than others? Why? Check that your children know which beaters are 'safe' for each instrument.

Try chanting these jingles in loud voices, choosing instrumental sounds to accompany them. The children might play the rhythm of the words, play on the strong beats (see page 46), punctuate the chant at appropriate places, or play continuously as a background to the chant. Discuss what would be suitable. Some ideas are given but ignore them if the children have their own.

Jingle jangle,
Silver bangle,
You look cute
From every angle.

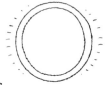

●Accompany with jingles and triangles.

Bang-bang-bang,
Eat brown bread,
I saw a sausage
Fall down dead.

●Tap out the rhythm of the words on drums and tambours.

Firecracker
Firecracker
Boom!
Boom!
Boom!

●Try random bursts of firecracker sounds on clappers or woodblocks, and booms on drums and tambours.

Silence in court!
The judge is dead,
Someone has sneezed
And blown off his head!

●Tap a tambourine loudly on sneezed. End with a moment of silence.

fff

Play the *ppp* game again (see page 25), but this time the children each make a loud sound on their instruments, taking care not to distort the sound.

●Discuss whether the sounds made were loud or noisy. Can the children describe the difference between loud and noisy?

●Did the loud sounds remind the children of anything, e.g. a banging door, a breaking glass?

●Go round the circle again alternating quiet and loud sounds.

CHAOS CAFE – *photocopiable gamesheet*

A mouse, anxious to feed her large family, braves the hazardous journey across the floor of a cafe to reach a lump of cheese on the floor. To a small mouse, the sounds made by a yelling baby, a dropped tray, the scrape of a chair, are loud and frightening.

What you need
●Two copies of the gamesheet, two pencils
●A selection of instruments
●A screen

The game is for two children: one makes the cafe sounds using instruments or voice, the other traces the route taken by the mouse.

To play:
The player making the sounds decides on the route and before playing numbers the circles on his or her gamesheet in the order in which they will be played. The other player, behind the screen, numbers the sounds in the order he or she hears them played. Each sound source should only be stopped at once. When the cheese has been reached, compare the routes. Swap and play again.

Chaos cafe

brrr brrr brrr brrr

3 Getting louder and getting quieter

The children will have experienced the effect of a sound getting louder – train approaching, mum shouting at them to get up as she walks upstairs, a kettle coming to the boil, one person talking then others joining in. But they may not have thought about how the sound gets louder.

Exploring

Ask the children to think of some situations where sounds get louder. Can they explain what is happening in each case to make the sound get louder?

●You can introduce the term *crescendo*, which means getting louder, and ask them what type of crescendo is being made.
After discussion you will probably arrive at these three types of crescendo achieved by

1 Using more effort
2 Joining in (where the number of people or things making the sound is increased)
3 Getting nearer to the sound source

In the same way talk about situations where sounds get quieter. What is happening this time?

●The musical term for getting quieter is *diminuendo*. Try sorting the situations into:

1 Using less effort
2 Dropping out (where the number of people or things making the sound get fewer)
3 Going away from the sound source

Signs and signals

Before you start the activities below, agree on some hand signals to use in conducting. You might point to a person or group to start a sound, and make a cutting motion to stop it. For a crescendo you might put your palms together in front of your chest and move your hands apart – slowly or more quickly according to the speed of the crescendo. Do the opposite to indicate a diminuendo.

USING MORE EFFORT

Voice and body sounds

●Try making a crescendo hum. Let the children take turns to hum quietly, get louder by putting more effort into the humming, and stop at an agreed signal. Try with a group.

●Change to a body sound or a sequence of them repeated.

CLAP STAMP CLAP STAMP CLAP STAMP

Singing together

Sing some of your favourite songs, starting quietly and getting louder. Try *She'll be coming round the mountain* or *Bananas in pyjamas.*

●Sing this phrase quite slowly, starting quietly and ending loudly.

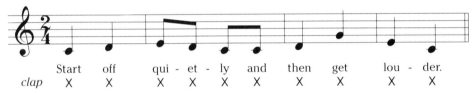

●For a more gradual crescendo, repeat the phrase a few times, getting louder all the time. Take care not to get faster.

●Add a body sound – clap and sing the words together. Try other sounds, but continue to sing the words.

●When the children know the rhythm really well they can make just the body sound. Keep it slow.

Instrumental sounds

●Talk about what has to be done to increase the volume when playing an instrument, e.g. shake, tap or blow harder.

●Pass an instrument round a circle of children and ask each to make a sound on it that is louder than the one before. Start off very quietly and stop as soon as the sound begins to distort.

●Let them experiment as they did with vocal and body sounds above. Sing *Start off quietly* again, and this time let one or two children select and play an instrumental crescendo through it.

USING LESS EFFORT

Voice and body sounds

Repeat the previous exercises, this time starting loudly and getting quieter.

- Take turns to hum loudly and then get quieter. Try it with a group.
- Try other sounds – sirens, engines, etc.
- Make a diminuendo with repeated words, e.g. 'goodbye, goodbye, goodbye.'
- Make a diminuendo with repeated body sounds:

Singing together

Sing some of your favourite songs, starting loudly and getting quieter. Try *The bear went over the mountain,* or *The runaway train.*

- Change the words of *Start off quietly* to *Start off loudly and then get quieter.* Add body sounds as above.

Start off loud – ly and then get quie - ter.

VC

We've had a lovely day

We've had a love - ly day at school

And now it's time to say, 'Good-bye un - til we

Repeat, getting quieter each time

meet a - gain, Go safe - ly on your way.'

I often finish the day with this goodbye song. The children repeat the last line, getting quieter and quieter until no sound can be heard – a wonderful moment of peace in which you can, quietly, remind them to take home their pullovers and reading books …

Instrumental sounds

- Pass an instrument round a circle of children, and ask each child to make a sound on it which is quieter than the one before. Start off quite loudly.
- Sing the phrase below repeatedly, getting quieter all the time. Let one or two children choose instruments to accompany it (playing continuously or matching the rhythm of the words).

Gra - dual - ly our play-ing gets much qui - et - er.

JOINING IN

Voice and body sounds

Make a circle of eight children and ask for a word or short phrase to chant, e.g. name of teacher, or school. A conductor stands inside the circle and points to the children in turn, bringing them into the chant one by one until everyone is chanting.

●What do the listeners notice? (The crescendo will not be as dramatic as those made with more effort, and you may need to remind the chanting children not to get louder individually.)

Singing together

Dee-di-diddle-o

VC

1. All a - lone sit - ting on the floor,

Dee - di - did - dle - o, here's one more.

2 Two fine friends sitting on the floor,
   Dee-di-diddle-o, here's one more.

3 Three fine friends sitting on the floor,
   Dee-di-diddle-o, here's one more.

●First learn the song.

●The child who starts off the song points to a friend to join him or her on the floor. That child chooses the next child, and so on.

●Everyone sings.

More songs to sing

Look for cumulative songs to which you can add instrumental sounds in a joining-in crescendo:

●Try *Johnny taps with one hammer* – select an instrument to make the hammer sound, and let a child tap out the strong beats throughout the verse (see page 46). Another child on another instrument joins in on the second verse, and so on.

●Let the children find a mowing sound to play during *One man went to mow*, and accumulate the mowing machines as the song progresses.

●Add the sound of tramping feet to *The ants go marching one by one*.

Instrumental sounds

●Accompany *Dee-di-diddle-o* with instruments – Let the children join in two by two – one child singing, the other playing the ostinato on a tuned or untuned percussion instrument (four times per verse):

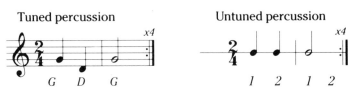

Tuned percussion   Untuned percussion

G   D   G   1   2   1   2

DROPPING OUT

Voice and body sounds

●Chant a name or phrase all together. Let a conductor point to the children one by one to stop chanting.

●Slap knees all together. Let a conductor stop the children one by one.

Singing together

There are several well-known songs in which singers and instruments can drop out, giving the effect of a diminuendo. Try singing *Five little speckled frogs* to an accompaniment of guiros or scrapers, or *Ten fat sausages sizzling in the pan* with sandpaper blocks or crinkly wrappings from inside chocolate boxes.

Five little monkeys

1. Five lit - tle mon - keys boun - cing on the bed,

One fell off and bumped his head,

Mam - ma called the doc - tor and the doc - tor said,

'No more mon - key busi - ness boun - cing on the bed.'

2 Four little monkeys bouncing on the bed,
One fell off and bumped his head,
Mamma called the doctor and the doctor said,
'No more monkey business bouncing on the bed!'

3 Three little monkeys...

● Decide together on a sound to represent the bouncing bedsprings – perhaps guiros, or rulers (one end is pressed firmly against a desk top, the other, which sticks out, is flicked to make a sound like a spring).

● Choose five children to play, one dropping out at the end of each verse until only one child is left. Start with ten monkeys and drop out in twos to make the diminuendo more obvious.

Signs and signals

● The musical sign for getting louder – the crescendo sign – is:

Draw one on a large piece of card. Turn it upside down. What is it now?

● Now that they have experienced making sounds get louder and quieter, can they think of any other ways of drawing a crescendo or diminuendo? For instance a joining-in crescendo might look like this:

COMING AND GOING – *photocopiable gamesheet*

Preparation
● Ask the children to think of situations in which a sound seems to get louder as it gets nearer – a fire engine approaching the listener, or the listener approaching a stationary sound such as a bird singing in a tree or a busker playing on a street corner. What happens as the sound maker or the listener goes away?

● Send someone with noisy shoes along the corridor or to the far end of the hall and ask them to walk towards the listening children. What do the listeners notice? Does the walker notice an increase in sound?

What you need:
● One copy of the gamesheet per child
● A selection of instruments

To play:
Show the children the gamesheet and talk about the pictures. The children pretend that they are the figure in the centre of each picture. How would the approaching and departing car/sleigh/footsteps sound to them? Can they select and play an instrument to give an impression of the crescendo and diminuendo of sound. There is a space on the sheet for them to make up their scenario.

Coming or going

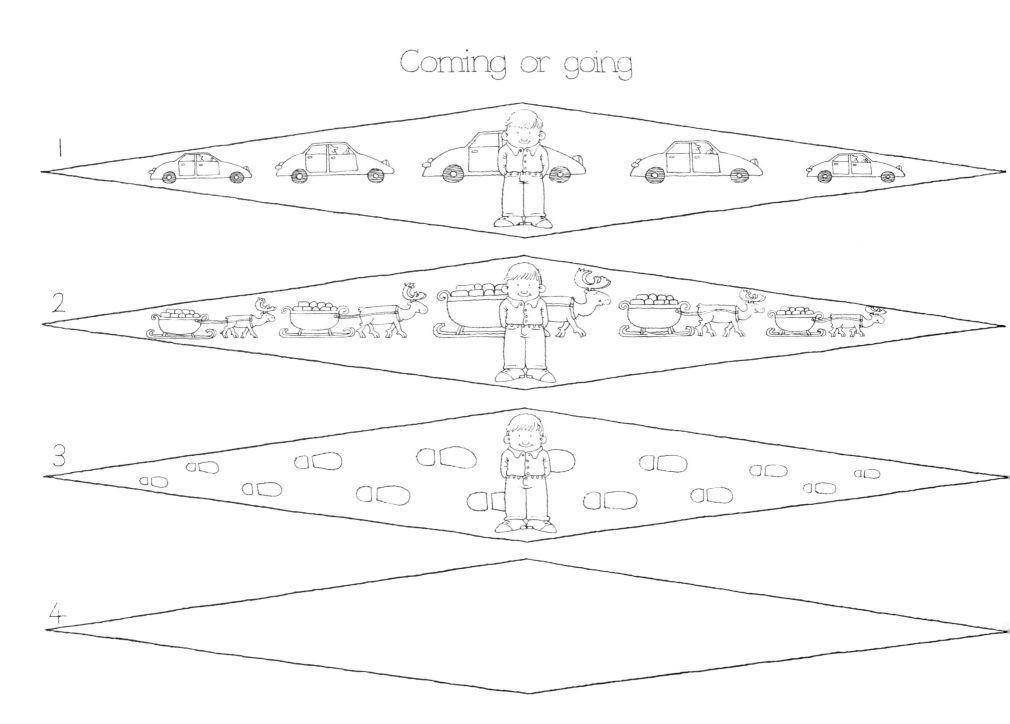

4 Loud and quiet together

This final unit contains a story and a gamesheet. These allow the children to practise all the skills gained in the previous units.

The two birds and the Raja

Traditional, retold by Helen East

●Tell the story then discuss where sound effects can be introduced to enhance the storytelling, for instance at *.

●First discuss what you are going to use to make each sound. Try out each suggestion before settling for your final choice. Pay particular attention to the volume of each sound. Will it be loud or quiet? Will it get louder or quieter, or will it remain the same? Will there be combinations of loud and quiet sounds? For instance in the scene where the ants tickle the elephants, there could be an interesting contrast between quiet tickling sounds and loud stamping sounds.

●The chants (in italics) can be accompanied with instrumental or other sound effects or they can remain simply as vocal chants. There are opportunities in the storyline for the chants to be heard getting louder (for instance, when the ants listen to the sound of the approaching bird), getting quieter (as the bird/ants/river set off down the road to the palace), and staying the same (when the bird plays her drum to call out the ants then the river).

There were two birds who lived in a tree, and they were happy as the day was long. One would start to sing, and the other would answer. Then the second would begin and the first would follow on. *

One day the Raja came riding by and he heard their song. Straight away he wanted those birds in a cage and that music in his palace. So his servants threw nets, but they didn't catch both the birds. They only caught one, and him they took back to the palace. So one bird was left alone in the tree and she was very sad. But she was also very determined.

'I'm not going to leave my friend in that palace!' she said to herself, 'I'm going to rescue him!'

So she made herself a little drum to help keep her spirits up, and off she set down the road to the palace, playing on her drum –

Tacketa tacketa tacketa tacketa

Now further along the road, there was a great mound of ants all running here and there. Away in the distance they heard the sound of the little bird's drum approaching them, and they stopped what they were doing and listened. *

When the little bird came up to them, they all called out to her, 'Where are you going to, little bird?'

'I'm going to the Raja's palace to rescue my friend,' she answered.

'Oh,' said the ants, 'may we come too? Maybe we can help you, little though we are.'

'Very well,' said the bird, 'you'd better climb into my right ear.'

So the ants all climbed into the bird's right ear and off they all went down the road, the bird playing her drum –

Tacketa tacketa tacketa tacketa

and all the ants answering from inside her ear –

Timitimi di timitimi di timitimi di timitimi di

Now even further along the road, a wide, wide river rolled on its way to the sea. Far, far in the distance, the river heard the little bird and the ants approaching and it stopped rolling and quietly listened. *

When the bird and the ants arrived beside it, the river looked up and asked, 'Where are you going to?'

'We're going to the Raja's palace to rescue my friend,' said the bird.

'May I come with you?' asked the river.

'Very well,' said the bird, ' but you'll have to get into my left ear. So the river made itself very small and slipped into the bird's left ear. And then off they all went together, away down the road to the Raja's palace, the bird playing on her drum –

Tacketa tacketa tacketa tacketa

and the ants in one ear answering –

Timitimi di timitimi di timitimi di timitimi di

and the river singing in its smooth rolling voice from the other ear –

Teum da da teum da da teum da da

And so they went on until at last they came to the Raja's palace. The little bird walked boldly up the steps and marched into the great hall where the Raja was sitting on his throne. She went up to him and said, 'I want my friend back!'

And the Raja loudly laughed, 'Ha ha ha ha ha! How dare this little bird come in here and speak to me like that. Take it and put it in with the elephants for the night. They'll trample it flat and that will be an end of its nonsense.'

So the servants threw the little bird in with the great big elephants in their stable. But as soon as the bird was alone she softly called to the ants in her right ear –

Tacketa tacketa tacketa

and the ants came swarming out –

Timitimi di timitimi di

And they ran all over the elephants' feet, they ran up the elephants' legs and over their backs and down along their trunks and in between their ears *. And they tickled and tickled and tickled, so that the elephants began to stamp and shake *. And soon they were blundering into each other, thudding into the sides of the stable, and trumpeting with all their might –

Whooooooo ooo whooooooo oooo

At last they could stand it no longer – they burst through the stable door, and off they all ran into the night . *

So the next morning when the servants came to find the little bird, instead of finding her trampled down, they found the stable trampled down, and all the elephants gone. They took the bird to the Raja and he was even angrier.

'How dare you come and chase away all my elephants!' he screamed. 'I'm going to put you somewhere where I can keep an eye on you.'

And he had the bird tied up to the end of his great big bed. All day he lay in his bed, and he ate and ate and ate. But he didn't give anything to the little bird. Then he lay down and he began to watch the bird, and as he watched his head began to droop and by and by he fell fast asleep. As soon as he was asleep, the bird played upon her drum –

Tacketa tacketa tacketa tacketa

and out from her left ear came the great rolling river –

Teum da da teum da da teum da da teum da da

And the river began to fill the room – little by little the Raja's bed began to float, then slowly it began to rise up and up, higher and higher on the rippling water *. Soon the Raja's nose went BUMP against the ceiling, and he woke up squashed flat against it – and the water still rising. *

'Help! Help! Help!' he called. Then he saw the bird.

'Little bird, you're the cause of all my troubles. Just *go away* and you can have *anything* you want.'

'Well,' said the bird, 'All I want is my friend back free with me.'

'Take him,' said the Raja, 'He's no use to me anyway – he hasn't sung a note since he arrived in the palace. Take him and go!'

So the bird took her friend and off they all went, the bird with her little drum –

Tacketa tacketa tacketa tacketa

her friend answering–

Tum dum tum dum tum dum tum dum

the ants saying –

Timitimi di timitimi di timitimi di timitimi di

and the river singing –

Teum da da teum da da teum da da teum da da

And ever after, the birds lived happy as could be in their tree, making music with the ants and the river.

Photocopiable gamesheet

The pictures describe some of the main events of the story – in the wrong order. They can be used in the music corner by individuals or small groups of up to four working together. The objective is to tell the story briefly in sound using a selection of instruments and vocal or body sounds, paying special attention to volume. There is a space at the bottom of each picture for the children to write in volume instructions, i.e. loud, quiet, in between, getting louder, getting quieter, or combinations of these. The pictures need to be sequenced and the children can do this either by numbering them from 1–6 in the top corners, or cutting them out and arranging them in the correct order.

The two birds and the Raja

The science of sound – *quieter and louder*

Voices

Humans and animals produce an enormous range of sounds with their voices. What produces the vibrations that make the sound waves? Help the children feel the vibrations in their voice boxes by asking them to touch their throats gently while humming. How can they make the hum louder? Ask one of the children to take a very deep breath and hum loudly for as long as he or she can. What happens as the breath runs out. When all the breath has gone can he or she still hum?

Amplification

Can the children think of more effective ways to make a hum travel to a listener – for example, by humming through cupped hands, or through a home-made megaphone (paper or card cone or tube), or through the water-filled balloon? Why can the hum be heard more clearly?

Musical instruments

Use percussion instruments with different sound qualities for further volume tests (try jingles, a tambour, a maraca, a wood block and a triangle). Make a chart like the one below to show the carrying properties of each instrument when the same amount of force is used to play it.

Instrument	Easy to hear	Hard to hear
(triangle)	✓	
(maraca)		✓

●Which instrumental sound seemed loudest. Can the children think why? (Look at the size, mass and shape of the instruments.)

Buildings

Which rooms in the school are noisy? Why are they noisy? Compare such things as size, flooring, furnishings, the type of activity taking place. Which are the quietest floor surfaces or coverings?

Footsteps

Can the children identify the various adults in the school by their footsteps? Describe the footsteps of some of the staff in terms of speed, lightness or heaviness of tread, and sound quality. What sort of shoes do members of staff wear? Make a set of shoes and sub-set into quiet and noisy shoes. Look at the soles of the shoes and relate the materials out of which they are made to the volume of sound they produce. Is it possible to walk noisily in 'quiet' shoes? Quietly in 'noisy' shoes?

Drums

Make drums out of a variety of containers – cardboard boxes, tins, plastic tubs. Which produce the loudest/quietest sounds? What factors, other than the materials they are made from, will affect the loudness or quietness of the sounds produced (e.g. force used to tap, type of beater, surface on which the drum rests). Can the children think of ways to control these extra factors so that the different types of material can be compared more accurately.

Beaters

Select one drum and try playing it with a variety of beaters – wood, rubber, felt, brush, plastic, etc. Discuss the sounds produced. Which produces the loudest sound, which the quietest? Why?

Care of the ears

Some jobs are noisy and can harm the ears unless suitable protection is worn. Find out how ears work. Make a series of loud crashes on a cymbal and ask the children to find ways of reducing the noise level (hands over ears, ear muffs, hat pulled down over ears, moving away from the sound source, and so on.)

Big and small vibrations

Large vibrations produce loud sounds, small vibrations produce quieter sounds. You might be able to see this size variation on some of your musical instruments. Tap a suspended cymbal hard and watch the vibrating rim. Then tap it softly and the children should be able to see a smaller movement of the rim. Scatter some chalk dust on the upper surface of the cymbal and watch it bound around with varying degrees of movement according to the force with which the cymbal is tapped. Pluck a guitar string firmly then gently, and observe the extent of the vibrations.

1 Slow and fast in contrast

This unit explores and contrasts fast and slow movement, then sound. The children are helped towards an understanding of tempo with reference to their immediate environment. The children are also asked to consider tempo in terms of regular and irregular patterns of sound and movement.

Exploring

Have a slow half hour in which the children do everything they have to very slowly: speaking, reading and writing, standing up and sitting down, getting out and putting away equipment.

●Use the opportunity to encourage them to take care with everything they do.

●Discuss how this slow pace affects their mood – do they feel peaceful, happy, irritated, impatient?

●Talk about things that move slowly:

slugs   sloths   the sun   the hands of a clock   clouds

●Let the children singly or in small groups try to give an impression of one of these through movement.

Have a fast half hour in which the children try some of these activities:

●Ask the children to repeat an action at a fast tempo, e.g. clap, slap knees, wink, open and shut their mouths. Can anyone flap a hand so quickly that it looks blurred?

●Use a sand timer or stop watch to time activities like these over a minute: the number of times they can write 0 – 10, write their name, bounce and catch a ball, and so on.

●How does the fast pace affect their mood – do they feel happy, rushed, excited?

●Talk about things that can move quickly:

cars   motor bikes   bluebottles   aeroplanes
a big dipper   racehounds   bullets   rockets

●Which children like the sensation of speed? When is it fun? When is it scary?

Slow motion replay

Let a child choose an action which is usually done quickly (cleaning teeth, brushing hair, running for a bus) and mime it in slow motion. Can the others guess what is happening?

Fast forward

Most of the children will have seen speeded up video film. Talk about the various stages of getting up in the morning: waking, stretching, getting out of bed, washing, etc. Ask them to mime each stage first at normal speed then speeded up. Put the whole thing together in fast motion being careful not to miss out any stage. Ask for other scenes to mime.

Voice and body sounds

Sloths and squirrels

Help the children to recognise and perform variations in tempo. Divide the class into sloths and squirrels. Let them imagine they are high up in the branches of a rainforest. Make the following sounds one at a time either quickly or slowly. Ask the children to listen and join in with the slow sounds if they are sloths, and with the fast sounds if they are squirrels. Aim initially for a big contrast of speed.

I'm moving along a branch (*slap hands on knees*)
I'm brushing past leaves (*rub hands together*)
I'm washing myself (*licking sound*)
Ooooh! I need a good scratch (*scratching sound*)
I'm thirsty (*lapping sound*)
Now I'm hungry (*chewing sound*)

●Let the squirrels take a turn at being sloths and vice versa and let a child initiate the sounds.

●Introduce another animal which would move at an in-between speed, e.g. a chimpanzee.

Using poems and jingles

Read *The appointment* and ask the children what would be an appropriate tempo for each verse.

The appointment   *VC*

We ran and we rushed,
Our faces were flushed,
Our legs were tired,
Our bodies perspired,
We walked through the door
At a quarter to four,
With lots of time to spare.

The next time we dallied,
We shillied and shallied.
We kicked a tin,
And made a din.
We walked through the door
At a quarter past four,
Late, late, late!

The third time we walked
Quite briskly, and talked.
No kicks, no hops,
No looking in shops.
We walked through that
    door
As the clock struck four.
Right on time – HOORAY!

●Ask three children to say the poem taking one verse each. Ask the others to judge how well they manage the contrast of tempo.

Read each of these two poems first slowly and then quickly:

Slowly the tide creeps up the sand   *James Reeves*

Slowly the tide creeps up the sand,
Slowly the shadows cross the land.
Slowly the cart-horse pulls his mile,
Slowly the old man mounts the stile.

Slowly the hands move round the clock,
Slowly the dew dries on the dock.
Slow is the snail – but slowest of all
The green moss spreads on the old brick wall.

Chickety-chee   *VC*

Chickety-chee, chickety-chee,
Want to be free, want to be free,
Chickety-chack, chickety-chack,
Stay on the track, stay on the track.

●Which tempo feels right for each poem?
●Can the children add voice and body sounds to suit the tempo of each poem?
●Which of the sounds might have a regular pulse (e.g. plod of cart-horse, man's footsteps, the train). Which might be irregular (e.g. the wash of waves, the shadows).

Singing together

Talk about the appropriate speed or tempo for the songs you sing together. Contrast a slow lullaby with a fast train song for example. How does the tempo of the singing affect the way the children feel?

If you're happy and you know it

If you're happy and you know it clap like this,
If you're happy and you know it clap like this,
If you're happy and you know it then you surely want
    to show it,
If you're happy and you know it clap like this.

If you're tired and you know it clap like this . . .

If you're late . . .

If you're sad . . .

●Before singing each verse, ask the children about an appropriate tempo to suit the words.
●Make up your own variations with the children, and change *clap* to *play* if you want to use instruments.

The Hare and the Tortoise
VC

This popular story gives the children the chance to experiment with fast and slow sound effects and actions. The *thumpas* of Hare's swift feet can be accompanied with rapid taps on the thighs. Slowly thump the chest for Tortoise's plodding *dib dobs*. Supplement or replace the body sounds with instruments if you like. Encourage the children to keep together if they can, though this will be tricky when Hare is running very fast.

●Discuss variations of tempo. Hare, after consuming twenty carrots, would slow down his running speed considerably. Tortoise would maintain a slow, steady pace from start to finish. Hare's final sprint would be frantic.

●The words the animals sing are sung to the first half of *Twinkle twinkle little star* (see below). Ask the children to suggest a tempo to suit each occasion when the animals sing.

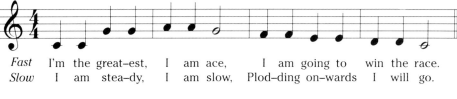

Fast   I'm the great–est,   I am ace,   I am going to   win the race.
Slow   I am stea–dy,   I am slow,   Plod–ding on–wards   I will go.

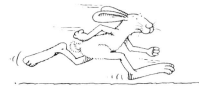

Hare was a big-headed sort of fellow. Anything you could do, he could do better. Who grew the longest carrots? Hare. Who could jump the furthest? Hare. Who had the biggest head? Hare!

One sunny afternoon the animals were sitting around trying to think of something to do. Hare was being a nuisance, because he only wanted to play the games he was sure to win. 'I know,' he chortled, 'Let's have a race.'

The animals groaned.

'Oh come on, spoilsports, I'll give you a start,' said Hare.

'You'll still win,' grumbled Hedgehog.

'Well what do you suggest?' snapped Hare, 'We can't sit around doing nothing.'

'What about a marathon?' came a quiet voice from the back.

'Now you're talking, Tortoise,' said Hare, 'Where do we start?'

Hare leaped up and started jogging on the spot.

'We start right here,' said Tortoise. 'We run through the wood, across the carrot field, past the pond, round the haystack and back here again.'

'Piece of cake,' chuckled Hare. 'Line up here for the marathon.'

Only Tortoise shuffled forward to join Hare.

'Just you and me, old chap,' said Hare, 'See you next week!'

And he shot off down the woodland track –

Thumpa thumpa thumpa . . .

Hare reached the tall fir tree before Tortoise had even moved. He turned round and shouted, 'Come on, slowcoach,' and sang:

I'm the greatest, I am ace,
I am going to win the race.

Then he flicked his tail and shot off again –

Thumpa thumpa thumpa . . .

Tortoise wasn't at all upset by Hare's arrogance. Slowly he lifted himself up onto his stumpy legs and began to plod towards the fir tree. As he went he sang:

I am steady, I am slow,
Plodding onwards I will go.

And he did just that –

Dib dob, dib dob, dib dob . . .

Hare soon reached the carrot field. He stopped to see if the carrots were ready to eat. The first one he pulled up was perfect – long, fat and juicy. Nineteen carrots later Hare was feeling a bit full. He set off again, but not as quickly as before –

Thumpa thumpa thumpa . . .

Seeing an inviting clump of grass by the side of the road, Hare slowed down. Glancing back along the road to check that there was no sign of Tortoise, he settled down for a snooze. His eyes were still closed two hours later when Tortoise came plodding past. Tortoise smiled to himself as he sang quietly:

I am steady, I am slow,
Plodding onwards I will go.

When Hare woke up it was getting chilly. He stretched and looked back down the road. Pausing only to straighten his whiskers he set off again towards the pond –

Thumpa thumpa thumpa . . .

He stopped to gaze at his reflection then headed towards the haystack. The sun was setting as he rounded the corner. He was amazed to hear a voice in front of him singing:

I am steady, I am slow,
Plodding onwards I will go.

There, just a few steps from the finishing post was Tortoise. Hare was horrified. He could not be beaten by a tortoise. He sprang forward and sprinted as fast as he could towards the little plodding figure. Faster and faster he ran –

Thumpa thumpa thumpa thumpa thumpa . . .

Tortoise was resting in his shell when Hare crossed the finishing line. 'What kept you, Hare?' he murmured.

The other animals stood around chuckling. Sadly Hare turned away to go home. 'Never,' he said to himself, as he limped down the track, 'Never again will I think I'm the greatest.'

Instrumental sounds

The first part of this unit was concerned with fast and slow movements. Some children if asked to play an instrument quickly, think they are required to make a single rapid playing action. They might for example, lunge towards a drum to make one quick tap. Requested to play slowly, they might make one slow, loose and ineffective shaking movement on a maraca. Help them to understand that here we are concerned with the speed with which a sound is repeated or moves on to a different sound.

Exploring

Let the children take turns to choose an instrument and imitate one of the following sounds:

– someone walking slowly along a gravel path
– someone in high heels running down a road

– Big Ben slowly chiming midnight
– a fast ticking alarm clock

– a fire alarm
– a fog horn

– someone walking reluctantly to bed
– someone running downstairs to open the door.

SLOW, IN-BETWEEN, FAST – *photocopiable gamesheet*

Talk about each strip. Which of the three pictures depicts the slowest speed, which the in-between speed and which the fastest? Illustrate with vocal sounds and actions. Put copies of the gamesheet in the music corner with a few instruments, including pitched percussion.

To play:
The children play in pairs. One child chooses a strip and makes an instrumental sound to represent each of the pictures. (Encourage the children to think about instrumental timbre, pitch and volume, as well as speed.) The other child listens and decides which order the pictures have been played in. He or she numbers them and plays them back.

The space below each picture can be used for drawing a graphic score. Can the children find a way to draw each of the sounds so that the various speeds are represented?

Slow, in-between, fast

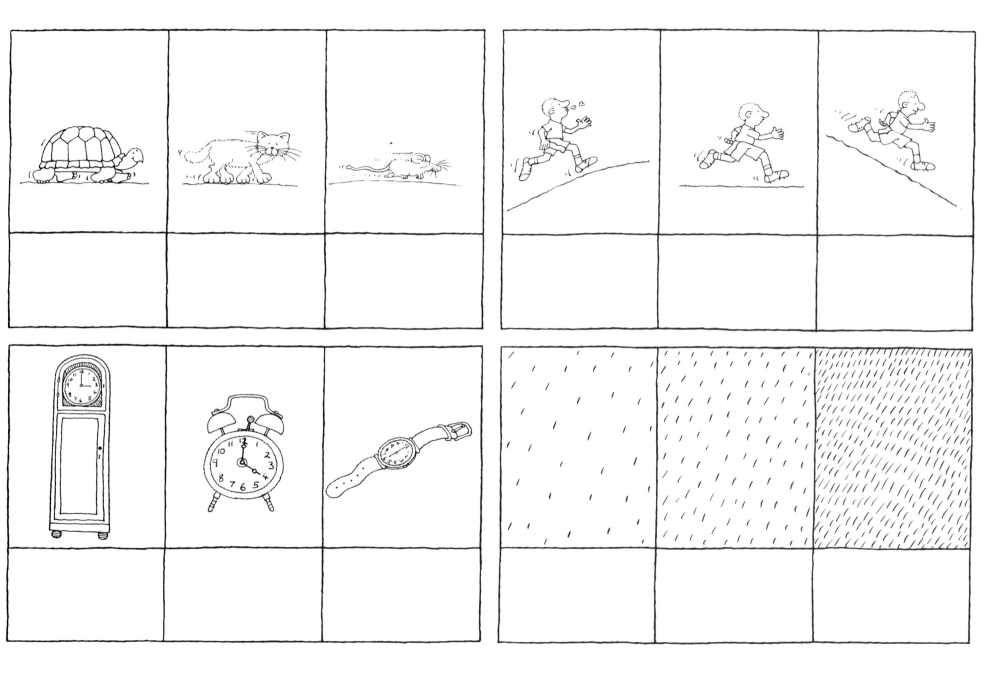

2 Maintaining a steady pulse

The rhymes and songs in this unit are all chosen to give your children practice in setting up and maintaining a steady beating pulse whether it is fast, slow or in-between. The emphasis is on choosing a tempo to suit the feeling of the material.

Some of your children may feel the rhythm of the words more strongly than the underlying pulse or beat. Such children will want to clap or tap the syllables of the words. Children need to be able to recognise and perform both the beat and the rhythm of music. In this section we are concerned with the pulse or beat, so encourage your rhythm tappers to be aware of it and play it. Set a strong lead and ask them to watch as well as listen.

SLOW AND FAST IN CONTRAST

Invite the children to beat a steady, slow pulse as you say *Slowly slowly* together. They can clap, tap, or rock themselves on the beat. The symbol / indicates the beating pulse. Set a fast pulse for *Quickly quickly*. Once they are confidently matching a physical action to the beat, let them choose an instrumental sound to play on it.

    /   /   /   /
Slowly, slowly, very slowly
    /   /   /   /
Creeps the garden snail. ___
    /   /   /   /
Slowly, slowly, very slowly
    /   /   /   /
Up the wooden rail. ___

    /   /   /   /
Quickly, quickly, very quickly
    /   /   /   /
Runs the little mouse. ___
    /   /   /   /
Quickly, quickly, very quickly
    /   /   /   /
Round and round the house. ___

GROUPING INTO TWOS, THREES AND FOURS

These clapping games will give the children more practice in beating the pulse of a chant or song. To begin with, just clap the beat throughout. When they are confidently doing this, they can then go on and group the beat into twos, threes or fours by giving an emphasis to the first beat in each group. This is a good exercise for helping children to feel these groupings which are an integral part of much of our music. In written music the first beat in the group is marked by a vertical line placed before it – this is called a barline. A double barline marks the end of the music.

One, two, buckle my shoe

    /   /   /   /
One, two, buckle my shoe,

    /   /   /   /
Three, four, knock at the door,

    /   /   /   /
Five, six, pick up sticks,

    /   /   /   /
Seven, eight, lay them straight.

    /   /   /   /
Nine, ten, start again.

1 Clap or tap knees throughout on the beats. They are marked /

2 Accompany with a **two** pattern e.g. slap knees then clap, making the slap louder:

    /   /   /   /   /   /
slap clap **slap** clap **slap** clap

3 Ask the children to select two contrasting sounds (body or instrumental) to make into a two pattern, e.g. claves and jingles. Divide into two groups.

Juba this and Juba that

/ / / /
Juba this and Juba that
/ / / /
Juba killed a yellow cat,
/ / / /
Juba up and Juba down,
/ / / /
Juba running all around.

1 Clap or tap throughout.

2 Group the children in pairs facing each other and let them make up a simple **four** pattern, of which the first beat is the loudest, e.g. slap knees, clap, then slap partners hands twice.

3 Ask the children to select two instrumental or mouth sounds to replace the body sounds. Practise at a slow tempo at first then build up the speed.

Pat-a-cake

/ / / / / / / / / / /
Pat-a-cake, pat-a-cake, ba – ker's man, ____
/ / / / / / / / / / /
Bake me a cake as fast as you can. ____
/ / / / / / / / / /
Pat it and prick it and mark it with B, ____
/ / / / / / / / / /
Put it in the o - ven for ba- by and me.

Make up a **three** pattern: slap knees then clap hands together twice, or (in pairs) clap then slap partner's hands twice. Keep it slow.

Encourage the children to make up clapping patterns to other jingles.

The hippo munch

Tamar Swade

I'm a big hip-po-po-ta-mus with a big— bot-to-mus,

And a ve-ry big head. I shuf-fle a-long from

side to side I can o-pen my mouth up

e-ver so wide as I munch my whole–meal bread.

One two, one two, One two, one two.

● Sing the song together slowly, and add sounds and actions on the beat.

More songs to sing

Discuss the tempo of songs you sing together – what feels right? Sing *The runaway train* at a slow tempo, then a fast tempo – how does it feel? Sing *Row row row the boat* quickly then slowly – how does that feel?

Instrumental sounds

The next poem contains the regular tempo of windscreen wipers, and the irregular tempo of falling raindrops. In the first verse the tempo is slow, in the second it is fast.

Wipers: let the children practise moving their arms at two different windscreen wiper speeds – slowly for the odd drops of rain in the first verse, and at double the speed for the downpour in the second verse. Ask them to find an appropriate instrumental sound for the wipers.

Raindrops: ask two small groups of children to make the sound of rain – fingernails on table tops or on drums and tambours. One group practises making intermittent plops (verse 1), the second practises the sound of a heavy shower (verse 2).

Driving in the rain   *VC*

Swish   swash

Drops on the   windscreen,

Swish   swash

Push the rain away.

Flicker-flacker Flicker-flacker

Shower on the windscreen,

Flicker-flacker flicker flacker,

Push the rain away. _____

●Chant the poem together. Let the two raindrop groups join in on their respective verses, while the rest of the class make the windscreen wiper movements and sounds.

Signs and signals

Ask the children if they can devise symbols to show the two different speeds of the raindrops and of the windscreen wipers. Here is one suggestion:

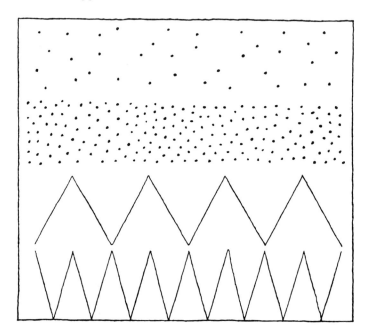

CONTRASTS – *photocopiable gamesheet*

Look at the pictures and talk about them. Are they depicting a fast or a slow situation? Recite the jingles at an appropriate speed. The children may need several practises to get the fast jingles up to speed.

Put copies of the sheet in the music corner along with a selection of percussion instruments. Ask the children to add instrumental accompaniments to match the pictures and chanting. The children can work singly or in pairs.

Discuss whether the accompaniments should be regular or irregular? They might decide to mark the beat by tapping a tambour throughout. Alternatively they might choose to play random shakes on a tambourine, or sustain one long sound throughout. Think about volume and instrumental timbre.

Contrasts

Pounding down the race course,
Heading for the line.
Who's the winner – number six?
No, it's number nine.

High up in the blue, blue sky,
A small white cloud goes drifting by.

Scritchety – scratch.
Scritchety – scratch,
The mice are having a football match.

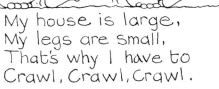

My house is large,
My legs are small,
That's why I have to
Crawl, Crawl, Crawl.

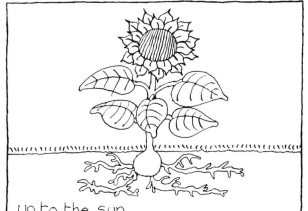

Up to the sun
Grow the small, green shoots.
Down through the earth
Grow the strong, white roots.

Zicker – zack, Zicker – zack,
Lightening, lightening,
Zicker – zack, zicker – zack,
Frightening, frightening.

3 Getting faster and getting slower

This unit looks at how the tempo can change during music – speeding up or slowing down – and how this affects the mood of the music. Like the previous unit, this one starts with movement then relates it to sound.

Exploring

Talk about times when movement speeds up, e.g.

– The children are playing chase in the playground. They speed up to avoid getting caught. How do they feel when they are putting on a sudden burst of speed?

– The children are out playing in the park, they reach a hill and run down it. How would they feel?

– A hamster starts off slowly in its wheel then gets faster and faster.

– The children are on a big dipper. It starts off on the level then suddenly whooshes down a steep gradient. How do they feel?

– The washing machine begins to spin, gradually getting faster.

Talk about times when movement slows down, e.g.

– an elderly person walking along meets a hill and slows down. How do they feel?

– a hamster trotting round on its wheel gets fed up and slows down.

– the big dipper comes to the end of its ride and slowly draws to a halt on the level. How do the children in it feel?

– a clockwork mouse winds down.

Mini-stories with sound

Ask the children in pairs to choose one of the situations above and extend it into a mini-story. One child tells the story while the other devises an accompaniment of sound effects – vocal, body or instrumental.

Hector ran impatiently around Josie waiting for her to throw the stick. 'Come on, come on' he seemed to say, 'hurry up and throw it. I can't wait much longer.' Then Josie raised her arm and threw the stick as far as she could across the grass. Hector bounded forward and raced after it.

Round and round in circles scuttled the clockwork mouse until its clockwork began to run down.

Signs and signals

Discuss how the tempo change in the mini-story could be represented on paper. Half the class can be involved in the activity while the other half listen and draw the sounds.

Voice and body sounds

I'm a hairy monster   VC

I'm a hairy monster creeping up on you.
Soon I'm going to catch you and pop you in my stew.
Faster and faster, I'm sniffing at your heels.
Faster and faster and faster . . . (*repeat ad infinitum*)
Ahhhhh!
What a tasty meal!

●Chant this jingle together and speed up the tempo during the telling.

Stair climbing   VC

I'm ninety-nine and I feel quite fit.
I like to walk and I swim a little bit.
But I really have to take my time
When I've lots and lots of stairs to climb.

●Slow down as you say the poem together. Add sound effects and actions, e.g. slap knees for footsteps.

Singing together

Cumulative songs such as *One man went to mow* (below), can be given a very exciting ending if the final verse is speeded up. The children sing happily all the way through knowing that at the end they are going to be allowed to let rip. Try others you know, e.g. *All in a wood, When I first came to this land, I know an old woman, The Ten Days of Christmas.*

One man went to mow

One man went to mow, Went to mow a

mea-dow.— One man and his dog, A bot-tle of pop, a

sau-sage roll, Old Mo-ther Ri - ley and her cow,

Went to mow a mea - dow.——

Two men went to mow,
Went to mow a meadow,
Two men, one man and his dog, a bottle of pop,
  a sausage roll, Old Mother Riley and her cow,
Went to mow a meadow. (*And so on*)

Follow my leader

Ask the children to look, listen and then join in with you as you clap, slap or click a slow, steady walking pulse. You can tell them that you are going to take them for a walk; they must keep up with you but they must not overtake.

●When the children are all playing with you, gradually speed up. Should anyone start to race away ahead of you, stop and start again.

●Let one of the children be the leader, stressing that it is the leader's job to keep everyone together, not win the race!

●Try the game with repeated vocal sounds, e.g. *la, la, la* . . .

●Let each child make a sound of their own choosing.

●Try it with instruments.

●Play the game again, this time setting off at a brisk pace and gradually slowing down.

JOURNEYS *photocopiable gamesheet*

Ask the children in pairs to describe these four scenarios in words and sounds. One child tells the story and the other, using either body or instrumental sounds, provides the sound effects. Quite a lot of skill is involved in putting the two parts together.

Journeys

start slowly   get faster   slow down   stop

4 Fast and slow together

Here, fast and slow sounds are combined and contrasted. At first the sounds have a different pulse from each other. Later they are controlled by a common pulse. It is quite difficult not to play in time with someone else. Two people walking along a pavement together tend to match their footsteps. If you are singing in a car during a rain shower, you will probably sing in time to the windscreen wipers.

FAST AND SLOW TOGETHER – UNRELATED

Exploring

Try the following games to get the children used to playing independently of each other. Choose two children at a time – one to play the fast sound, the other the slow one. Use voice, body and instrumental sounds. Tape and play back each activity.

- someone running for a bus – someone walking slowly along laden with heavy shopping
- a slowly tick-tocking grandfather clock – a rapidly ticking alarm clock
- an emergency siren – a slow church clock chime
- a runner panting quickly – someone sleeping and breathing slowly
- slowly stirring a pan of soup – rapidly chopping carrots
- someone sprinting along in a race – someone in a hopping race
- someone walking along a street – a small dog trotting along beside

●Can the children think of any more examples and demonstrate how they sound together.

Trains

Trains travel at various speeds depending on their function. Goods trains carrying heavy or dangerous freight are slow. Passenger trains which stop at suburban stations aren't as fast as express trains. Use these chants to illustrate the sound and speed of each type of train:

slow	freight train	chugga chugga chugga
in-between	suburban train	diddle-ee-dee diddle-ee-dee
fast	express train	wisha-washa-wisha-washa

●Accompany with body sounds, e.g. thigh slaps for the freight train, tap fingertips on palm for the suburban train, and swish palms together in circles for the express.

●Ask the children to match the trains to instrumental sounds and add these to the accompaniment of the chants.

●Now divide the class into two. Half the children imagine they are on a suburban train. They chant, make body sounds or use instruments to accompany themselves. The rest of the children pretend to be on an express train catching up on a parallel track. The express overtakes and disappears into the distance.

●Try again this time with the suburban and freight trains.

Clocks
VC

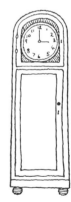

High clocks, low clocks,
Fast and slow clocks,
Big clocks, little clocks,
Tall and short.
Round clocks, square clocks,
In the open-air clocks.
Loud clocks, quiet clocks,
Clocks in glass.
Clocks to wake you,
Stir and shake you,
Wooden clocks, gold clocks,
Clocks of brass.

●Imitate the sounds of the different clocks. Sit in a circle and one by one start ticking at different speeds. Use voice, bodies and instruments.

FAST AND SLOW TOGETHER – RELATED

Using poems and jingles

In unit two, the children clapped a steady pulse to clapping games and jingles. They made two, three and four patterns out of the claps. In these jingles divide the children into two groups, one group to clap on each of the beats, and the other group to slap their knees or stamp on the first beat of each group, e.g. a two group:

```
STAMP          STAMP          STAMP
CLAP   CLAP    CLAP   CLAP    CLAP   CLAP    etc
```

One potato two potato

```
    *          *          *          *
  /   /   /      /      /   /      /
One potato, two potato,  Three potato, four ____
    *          *          *          *
  /   /   /      /      /   /      /
Five potato, six potato,  Seven potato more. ____
```

Group one claps on / while group two stamps on *

● Look back to page 46 and try *One two buckle my shoe* as a four pattern. Group one claps on / while group two stamps on the first beat of each line (*one, three, five,* and *seven*).

```
    *                      *
  /   /   /      /      /   /      /          /
One two buckle my shoe, three four knock at the door.
```

● Play the three pattern in *Pat-a-cake* with group one clapping on every beat marked / while group two stamp on the first beat of the group – marked *

```
    *          *          *          *
  /  /  /    /  /  /    /  /  /    /  /  /
Pat-a-cake, pat-a-cake, baker's man. ____
```

Using instruments

I hear thunder

```
    *          *          *          *
  /   /      /   /      /   /      /   /
I hear thunder,  I hear thunder,

    *          *        *              *
  /   /      /   /    /   /          /       /
Hark don't you?  hark don't you?

    *              *            *              *
  /       /      /     /      /       /      /
Pitter patter raindrops, pitter patter raindrops,

    *          *        *        *
  /   /      /   /    /  /  /    /
I'm wet through,  so are you.
```

● Use instruments to accompany this – a drum beat on *, and woodblocks or claves on /

● A third and faster set of beats can be introduced by tapping the rhythm of the words *pitter patter* in the fifth and sixth lines.

Singing together

Sing these two phrases several times until the children know them well. Clap, tap or shake the rhythm of the words. The two phrases fit together within the same controlling pulse, even though one *sounds* faster than the other.

Divide your class into two. Start one group off singing and slapping *I am tired* in a slow, weary manner. When the singing is well-established bring in the wide-awake group.

I am ti-red.   I am fee-ling wide a-wake.

Hey Jim along

Hey Jim a-long,_____ Jim a-long Jo-sie,

Hey Jim a-long,_____ Jim a-long Joe.

Hey Jim a-long,_____ Jim a-long Jo-sie,

Hey Jim a-long,_____ Jim a-long Joe.

2　Jump Jim along, Jim along Josie,
　　Jump Jim along, Jim along Joe.

3　Walk Jim along . . . 　　4　Run Jim along . . .

The pulse of this song is grouped in fours – there are four beats to each bar. Divide into two groups.

			Hey	Jim	a-long_____	
Group 1	Clap	*Verse 1 - 4:*	/	/	/ /	
Group 2	Stamp	*Verse 2:*	*			
		Verse 3:	*		*	etc
		Verse 4:	*	*	* *	

STARTING FROM NOW! – *photocopiable gamesheet*

This game is for three players. One, the starter, shakes the die and supervises the timing. The other two make the fast and slow sounds to describe the characters or objects on the gamesheet.

What you need
One copy of the gamesheet
● A die
● Six counters
● A digital timer
● A collection of instruments and two tempo cards, one marked FAST the other marked SLOW.

To play:
The starter shakes the die, finds the picture which corresponds to the number on the die and places a counter on it. He or she mixes up the two tempo cards and, without looking, gives one to each player. The players look at the picture to identify which character or object they are to represent and select an instrument which they think will best illustrate their fast or slow movement.

The starter says 'Starting from NOW!' and sets the digital timer in motion. The two players make their sounds *at the same time* (one fast, the other slowly), and are stopped by either the alarm on the timer, or, if there isn't one, by the child with the timer. The children put back their instruments and the die is shaken again. Each picture is played only once. The counters help to remind the players of the game's progress. The children can take turns to be the starter.

The game can be made more exciting by varying the duration of the playing. The starter can be allowed to choose anything between ten and thirty seconds and should set the timer according to his or her choice. There is no need to inform the players of the duration of play.

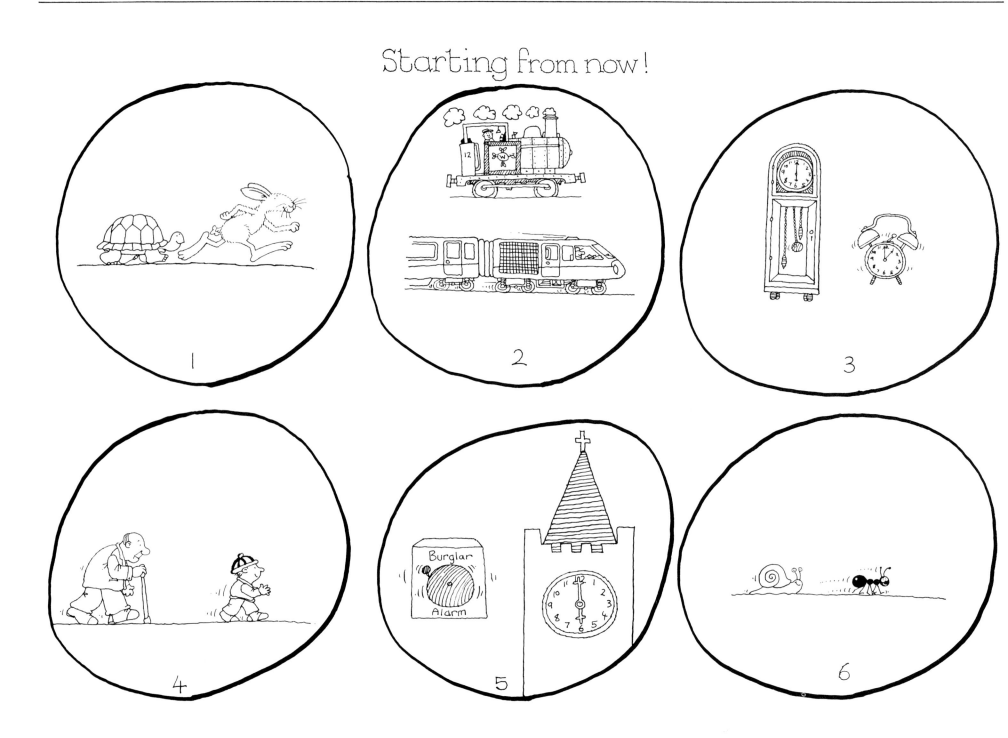

The science of sound – *faster and slower*

In considering faster and slower sounds, one has to bear in mind the frequency of the movement making the sound. A rapid triangle trill is caused by the player quickly tapping a beater across the corner of the instrument. The sound of slow footsteps results from slow walking. Experiment with movements repeated quickly and slowly and listen to the sounds they produce:

– clap
– cut paper
– click fingers
– run on the spot
– skip with a rope
– bounce a ball
– tap rulers together

Fast or slow?

One child comes to the front. The rest of the children close their eyes. The child does any of the activities described above either quickly or slowly. The listening children have to describe the speed of movement. Their judgement is based on what they hear. Alternatively, the children can cover their ears and guess, from watching the activity, whether the sound produced is fast or slow. They can decide whether or not they were correct by taking their hands from their ears and listening to the sound.

Fast or long?

Some sounds which appear to be continuous or sustained are in fact a succession of rapid sounds. They are produced by a sequence of rapid actions. You can demonstrate this with a simple clapping experiment.

● Ask half the class to clap as quickly as possible while the rest of the children listen. The listeners can close their eyes. The effect produced by a lot of children clapping quickly is that of a continous sound. Swap over.

● Experiment with various simple machines such as a football rattle, the winding mechanisms on clockwork toys, a hand beater. Turn them slowly and you will hear a succession of single sounds, turn them quickly and the fast sounds will blend to make one long sound.

● Can the children think of any environmental sounds which

demonstrate this principle? (Drumming rain, car engines, a cheering crowd, skate boards.)

Playing techniques

There is virtually no limit to how slowly sounds can be played in succession, but it can be very difficult to play or sing sounds quickly in succession. The children will learn a lot about how quickly or slowly they can repeat sounds by experimenting with their school percussion instruments. As the children experiment put the following questions to them:

● Is it easy to play several sounds quickly on this instrument? Playing an instrument quickly can present problems. Experiment with various tapping, scraping and shaking instruments to find the most effective way to play them quickly. Record the findings on a chart (see below). Are any of the sounds so rapid that they sound continuous?

Instrument	Best way to play quickly
△ /	tapping across the corner
(tambourine)	shaking
(drum)	drum fingers on skin

● Can you play quickly and quietly?
● Can you play quickly and loudly?
● Do you like playing quickly? Why? Why not?

Speed of playing in relation to pitch

Ask the children if they think that playing quickly changes the pitch of the sound. Does, for example, a sound get higher while it is being repeated quickly? (The children may have already learnt that high-pitched sounds have fast sound waves, low-pitched sounds have slow sound waves. It may be hard for them to grasp that sounds cannot be made higher or lower by repeating a sound more quickly. All that this does is produce sounds which are closer together in time).

To test this, put out two identical chime bars. One acts as a control, the other is played at different speeds. Invite a child to play one of the chime bars at varying speeds. Keep checking the pitch with the control bar.

1 High and low in contrast

This unit explores the extremes of high and low pitch.

Exploring

How high can your children speak/squeak?

●Ask each child to say his or her name in as high-pitched a voice as possible.

●Answer the register, count to ten, chant the days of the week, all in high-pitched voices.

●Pretend to be a class of mice. Vary the volume and tempo.

●Sing *Twinkle twinkle little star* in high-pitched voices.

Talk about high-pitched sounds the children hear:
– *in school*: screams in the playground, scraping chalk, computer and word processor bleeps, some voices
– *at home*: baby crying, some telephone and alarm bleeps, cat miaowing, violin, whistling
– *outside*: birdsong, yapping dogs, some car horns, brakes, sirens
●Ask the children to try imitating some of the sounds with their voices.

How low can your children speak?
●Growl register responses.

●Count to ten in low-pitched voices.

●Pretend to be a class of bears. Vary the volume and tempo.

●Sing *Twinkle twinkle* in very low-pitched voices.

Talk about low-pitched sounds the children hear:
– *in school*: rumble of trolleys, some voices
– *at home*: some machine noises, air lock in pipes
– *outside*: some vehicle noises, drumming rain, thunder, ships' hooters, rumble of roller boots and skate boards, fog horn
●Try imitating some of the sounds with voices.

What am I?

One child imitates something you have discussed which sounds very high, and the others guess what it is. Whoever guesses correctly thinks of a very low sound to imitate, and so on.

Voice and body sounds

This little piggy went to market

This little piggy went to market,
This little piggy stayed at home,
This little piggy had cheese on toast,
This little piggy had none.
And this little piggy went, 'Wee wee wee wee wee . . .'
All the way home.

●Ask the children what sort of voice the little pig might have – high or low-pitched? Try it both ways.

●Adapt the words of the rhyme so that it describes an animal with a lower-pitched voice, e.g. *This old bear went to market.*

The bogus-boo (extract)   *James Reeves*

The bogus-boo   Out from the park
Is a creature who   At dead of dark
Comes out at night –   He comes with huffling pad.
  and why?   If, when alone,
He likes the air;   You hear his moan,
He likes to scare   'Tis like to drive you mad.
The nervous passer-by.

●Ask the children to make low, creepy moaning sounds. They can be trembling, sustained, very short, loud or quiet. Use the sounds to accompany the poem.

●Say the poem again this time with high-pitched, spooky sounds – whines, wails and screeches.

●Which do the children think create a more spooky atmosphere? Do both high and low sounds work well together?

Music corner – make a large picture or model of the Bogus-boo, and display it in the music corner. Let the children experiment with a range of instruments to create a creepy sound environment for it.

Instrumental sounds

Unpitched percussion

Although these instruments are not intended to have clearly defined pitches, some can be clearly said to have higher pitches than others. For instance, small bells, or triangles do have a distinctively high pitch, whereas a large drum would be low-pitched in contrast. Others again will be very difficult to define in terms of pitch. Make sure that the children know they are not at fault if in the following activities they find it hard to say what pitch an instrument has.

●Set out a selection of instruments: Indian bells, a shaker or two, a guiro, jingles, a woodblock, a tulip block, one or more tambourines, triangle, drums and tambours of various sizes.

●Prepare three labels: HIGH, LOW, and HARD TO SAY. Put each label inside a large PE hoop on the floor. Let the children play and listen to each instrument and discuss its pitch. Place each in the appropriate set.

●Do any of the sounds remind the children of anything – what and why? Their answers may show an association with physical height, or something quite subjective.

Rabbit and Lark (extract)

James Reeves

'Under the ground
    It's rumbly and dark
And interesting,'
    Said Rabbit to Lark.

Said Lark to Rabbit,
    'Up in the sky
There's plenty of room
    And it's airy and high.'

●Let the children choose a few instruments from the high and low sets to provide a musical setting for each verse.

Pitched percussion

For the following games use an alto xylophone (wooden bars), as this is a good size for young children to play, and it has a clear, mellow tone. Until the children become skilled at identifying the differences in pitch, stand the instrument on its end, with the longer bars nearer the floor. Thus the low-pitched notes are physically low and the high-pitched notes are physically high.

Stand up sit down

Ask the children to listen and stand up or sit down on the floor according to whether you play the highest or lowest-sounding note of the xylophone.

Play high play low

Ask a child to look at the position of your hand and play either the lowest or highest-pitched note according to what you indicate – hand in the air means the highest, hand near the floor means the lowest.

Top or bottom?

Take off the highest and the lowest-pitched bars and invite a child to come out and pick up the higher-sounding bar. Let them check by placing the bars back on the xylophone and playing them.

Signs and signals

Experiment with simple scoring. On a piece of paper or card draw two horizontal lines, one high up, the other low down:

●Remove all but the two highest and lowest bars and choose a child to play them. Indicate which should be played by pointing to the higher or the lower line, or both together. Encourage the child to use a variety of playing techniques.

●Experiment further with elementary scoring. Draw two lines on a piece of card as before. Make up a short pattern of high and low sounds using two bars again (they need not be the highest and lowest, you could use two which are closer together in pitch), and discuss with the children how to represent the pattern on your score, e.g.

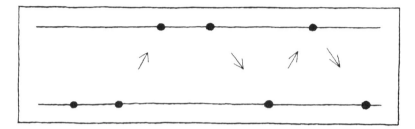

Work out with children how to show such things as volume, and tempo on your elementary score.

> **Music corner** – put the card and xylophone in the music corner and let the children, in pairs, play these pitch games themselves.

Tom and Jerry

Prepare as many tuned percussion instruments as you have available, by removing all but the lowest-pitched three or four bars from half the instruments and all but the highest-pitched three or four bars from the others. The low notes are for Tom, the high for Jerry. The children sit in a circle with an instrument each – alternating high and low.

●Talk about the sort of antics that Tom and Jerry get up to and think of a very short scene – perhaps Tom is creeping up on Jerry who is scurrying about collecting crumbs. Discuss how each would move. Can the children think of some music to play for each animal? Work round the circle letting each child in turn, play either their Tom or their Jerry music. Swap instruments.

●Think up a longer storyline. Let two children act it out while another two describe what is happening in sound. Make up your own scores to show what is happening.

Voices and instruments

Add high and low sound effects to these nursery rhymes. Use voices and instruments – pitched and unpitched. Ask the children to consider which sounds should be heard together and which separately, which should be fast and which slow, which loud and which quiet. Can the children make effective use of silences? (It is probably better if the teacher chants the nursery rhymes, as sympathetic pausing for sound effects will be required.) Try scoring the end results.

Hickory dickory dock

Hickory dickory dock,
The mouse ran up the clock,
The clock struck one,
The mouse ran down,
Hickory dickory dock.

●Chant or play a quiet, deep 'tick-tock' throughout. Discuss how you can make the sound of the mouse running up and down the clock. The chimes might be either low or high-pitched. Conclude with high-pitched vocal or instrumental squeaks.

Ride a cock horse

Ride a cock horse to Banbury Cross
To see a fine lady upon a white horse,
Rings on her fingers and bells on her toes,
She shall have music wherever she goes.

●Make low clicks with either mouths or a woodblock to represent the horse. Add high-pitched ringing instruments for the bells and rings.

An old man lives in lollipop land David Moses

1. An old man lives in Lol-li-pop Land, Sing

high, Sing low, *Sing high,* *Sing low,* And

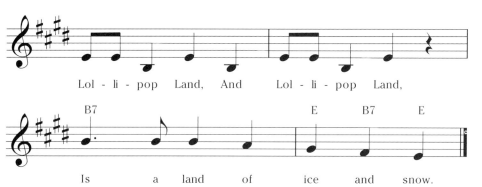

Lol-li-pop Land, And Lol-li-pop Land,

Is a land of ice and snow.

2 Now this old man has a bell to ring,
　Ring high, ring low, *Ring high, ring low,*
This funny old man, *This funny old man,*
Rings his bell wherever he goes.

3 His reindeer sleigh rides through the sky,
　Swoop high, swoop low, *Swoop high, swoop low,*
His reindeer sleigh, *His reindeer sleigh,*
Glides across the clouds of snow.

4 This reindeer sleigh has sacks of toys,
　Piled high, piled low, *Piled high, piled low,*
Those sacks on the back, *Those sacks on the back,*
Who they're for I do not know.

•Sing the song together and talk about the sounds in it – the bells, the sleigh gliding across the snow clouds, the sack of rattling toys.

•Find instruments for all of these sounds and where the words are repeated in italic, introduce the instrumental sounds.

•Add actions.

•Think about the pitch of other songs you sing together, e.g. *Twinkle twinkle little star* or *I hear thunder.* Try repeating a song a little higher or a little lower in pitch each time.

•Think about the type of voice in which to sing or say poems – light or heavy, loud or quiet, clipped or sustained.

PITCH IN! – *photocopiable gamesheet*

This is a simple game requiring high and low vocal sound effects. It is for two players. Before playing, talk about the eleven pictures on the gamesheet. Each one shows something which can produce both a high and a low sound. The cat, for example, can both purr and miaow. The car could sound a deep horn or screech to a halt with a squeal of brakes.

What you need:
Two dice and two cards, one marked HIGH and the other LOW.

To play:
Place the cards face down on the table. The first player shakes both dice and matches the number thrown to a picture on the gamesheet. He or she turns over one of the pitch cards. If it is marked HIGH the child makes a high sound effect, if it says LOW the effect should be low. The pitch cards are shuffled and placed face down ready for the next go.

The players can keep their die score secret so that after they have made their sound, their partners have to try to guess what has been imitated.

Variation:
The players share the die score. They take a pitch card each and make their sound *at the same time.* Thus if the score was six, one player could be gurgling like a baby and the other wailing.

Pitch in

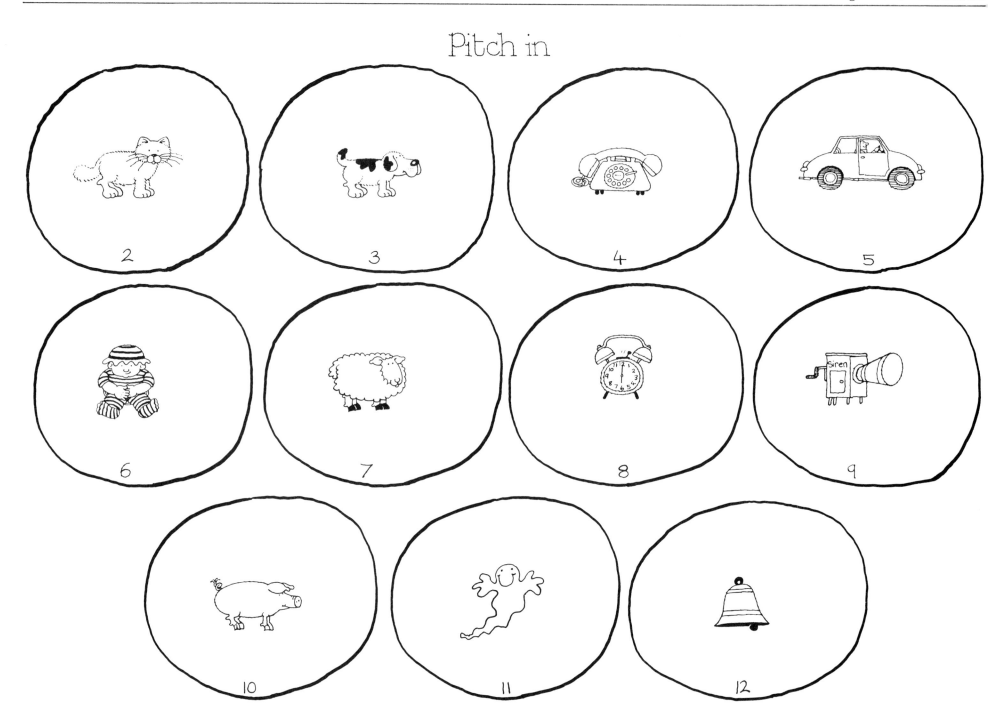

2 High, low, in-between

The first unit concentrated on extremes of pitch. Here, in-between pitches are added. By playing games based on three levels of pitch, the children will be able to create more subtle differentiations.

Vocal sounds

Telephone switchboard

Some phones ring, others beep. Practise both sounds at varying pitches – high, low and in-between.

●Make three labels – HIGH, LOW, and IN-BETWEEN – and hang them round the necks of three children.

●Start by pointing to LOW. The child wearing the LOW label makes the sound of a low telephone ring, and continues until you point to IN-BETWEEN. Finally point to HIGH.

●Ask the listeners if the telephones sounded higher each time.

●Next time start with the high ring and get lower. Let a child be the conductor.

●As the children get more confident and proficient vary the order and length of the telephone sequences.

●Let two or three telephones ring at the same time.

Signs and signals

Ask the children to think of ways to record some of the sequences, e.g.

brr brr	brr brr	
brr brr		brr brr
brr brr		

> **Music corner** – put the scores in the music corner, where the children can experiment with them using a variety of different ringing tones.

Goldilocks – *see next page*

Before you sing the song together, remind the children of the story and ask them which bear had the lowest voice, and which the highest? What was Mummy Bear's voice like?

●Practise saying, 'Who's been sitting in my chair' at three different pitches – a low growl, a high-pitched squeak, and an in-between voice.

●Practise 'Who's been eating my porridge?' and 'Who's been lying in my bed?' in the same way.

Signs and signals

How could the children write down each bear's words to show the pitch of them, e.g.

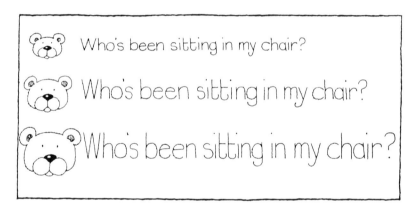

●Divide into three groups each representing one of the bears. Display the 'score' and let each group say its phrase when you point to that part of the score.

●What happens if you point to two phrases at the same time – or three?

●Let individual children take the parts of the three bears.

●Sing the song together. Ask the children what happens to the tune when each bear speaks in the chorus. Three children, each representing one of the bears, can sing the chorus. A few children can act out the story as the song is sung.

63

Goldilocks

Words: VC. Music: traditional

1. When Gol - di - locks went to the house of the bears, Sur - roun - ded by bu - shes and trees.

She tas - ted the por - ridge she found in the bowls, And ate it, the bears were not pleased, oh no, And ate it, the bears were not pleased.

Daddy Bear
Who's been eat - ing from my bowl?

Mummy Bear
Who's been eat - ing from mine?

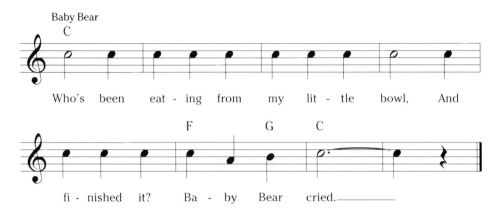

Baby Bear
Who's been eat - ing from my lit - tle bowl, And fi - nished it? Ba - by Bear cried.

2 Goldilocks found a house in the woods,
Surrounded by bushes and trees.
She tried all the chairs, then sat on the stool,
And broke it, the bears were not pleased, oh no,
And broke it, the bears were not pleased.
    'Who's been sitting on my chair?'
    'Who's been sitting on mine?'
    'Who's been sitting on my little chair,
    And broken it?' Baby Bear cried.

3 Goldilocks found a house in the woods,
Surrounded by bushes and trees.
She felt very tired, so she climbed into bed,
And slumbered, the bears were not pleased, oh no,
And slumbered, the bears were not pleased.
    'Who's been lying on my bed?'
    'Who's been lying on mine?'
    'Who's this sleeping in my little bed?
    'Get rid of her!' Baby Bear cried.

Final chorus
Daddy Bear gave a low growl,
Mummy Bear threatened to bite,
Baby Bear screamed at the top of his voice.
And Goldilocks shot off in fright!

Instrumental sounds

Ensure that the children can confidently identify the high and low-sounding bars of a xylophone by referring back to the exercises on page 59 if necessary. Remind the children of the voice work you did with *Goldilocks*.

●Choose three children to come out and select a note each from a xylophone (C – C') to represent the low growly voice of the father bear, another for the baby bear's high squeaky voice and a third in-between note for the mother bear's voice.

●Ask each child to sing and play on their chosen note the phrase 'Who's been eating from my bowl?'

●Choose another three children to come out and sing and play the next phrase, 'Who's been sitting on my chair?'

●What does it sound like when two of the bears sing and play together, or when all three play together. Experiment with different notes.

Signs and signals

Help the children to write simple scores of the bear's phrases at the three different pitches, e.g.

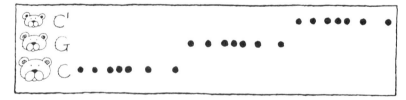

●By playing back their scores and discussing them, help the children to hear whether their scores are accurate enough – do they show how many notes to play, how fast, how loud or quiet?

●Let them make up their own sequences of high, low and in-between pitches and record them on paper.

> **Music corner** – put the finished scores and a suitable instrument with three beaters in the music corner, and let the children play them. They can work individually or in groups of three.

PICK A PIECE – *photocopiable gamesheet*

This game is for one person and it involves playing a sequence of sounds at varying pitches – high, low or in-between.

What you need:
One copy of the gamesheet. Mount it on card and cut out the boxes.
One pitched percussion instrument (either with the range of C –C', or with all but the C, G and C' notes removed) and two beaters.

To play:
Mix the cards and spread them out face down on the table. The player picks up four cards and (without looking) lays them down next to each other in the order they were picked. They might, for instance, run in this order: high, low, in-between, in-between. Physically position the cards up and down to indicate high, low and in-between:

Play the cards from left to right (use both beaters). Experiment with speed, volume and rhythm.

●After practise, the game can be extended by playing not one note but several for each of the cards. This will involve thinking about a rhythmic pattern for the notes which stay the same, and working out how to score this.

●Extend the game further with older children by making a set of cards for each note from C – C' (C D E F G A B C').

Pick a piece

high	high
in - between	in - between
low	low

3 Getting higher and getting lower

In this unit the children listen to and practise rising and falling sequences. These may take the form of slides or regular step-by-step movement. Encourage the children to draw the shape of the rising or falling patterns in the air using hand and arm gestures.

RISING AND FALLING SLIDES

Exploring vocal sounds

Talk about machines which speed up and slow down e.g. cars, washing machine spinners, liquidisers.

●Ask the children to imitate the sounds vocally. How high can their voices rise? How low can they fall?

(These exercises are particularly good for those children who have difficulty singing in tune. Let such children choose their own starting pitch and rise and fall from there.)

Mini-stories and sounds

Make up a mini-story about a machine. Ask individual children to provide the sound effects vocally, e.g.

> Terry was making meringues. The three egg whites wobbled in the bottom of the bowl. Terry switched on the liquidiser and gradually increased the speed. When the egg whites had become stiff and shiny, he switched to a slower speed.

Exploring instrumental sounds

Put out a mix of conventional and improvised instruments and let the children experiment to find ways of producing up or down slides on them, e.g.

●Twang an elastic band and stretch it at the same time.
●Blow up balloons and let the air escape by pinching and stretching the exit.
●Listen to the sound of a bottle being filled with water.
●Swanee whistles are ideal for demonstrating slides.

Accompany these poems and stories with vocal or instrumental slides. Vary the speed, volume and duration of the slides where appropriate and use body movements to reinforce the concept of moving from low to high, high to low. Encourage the children to use as much expression and imagination as they can in choosing sounds, and make scores of the results.

Diddly diddly dumpty
The cat ran up the plum tree.
Half a crown to fetch him down.
Diddly diddly dumpty.

Blast off!   *VC*

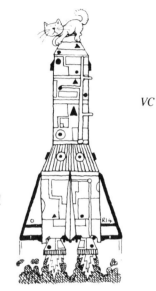

Smoke billows
Flames spurt
Engines roar
Ears hurt
10 9 8 7 6 5 4 3 2 1 ZERO. LIFT OFF!
Ground shakes
Crowd cheers
Rocket climbs
And disappears.

Coming up   *VC*

Bert was at the top of the ladder. Tessa was at the bottom.
Bert was mending the window frame. Tessa was helping.
'Throw up the saw, Tessa,' said Bert.
'One saw coming up,' said Tessa. ✲ 'Thanks,' said Bert.
'Throw up the hammer, Tessa,' said Bert.
'One hammer coming up,' said Tessa. ✲ 'Thanks,' said Bert.
'Throw up the sandpaper, Tessa,' said Bert.
'Sandpaper coming up,' said Tessa. ✲ 'Thanks,' said Bert.
'Throw up the tin of green paint, Tessa,' said Bert.
'One tin of green paint coming up,' said Tessa. ✲
'Oops, missed,' said Bert. ✲ 'YUK!' said Tessa.

●Add slides where you see ✲

Signs and signals – *Warnings*

There are several road warning signs which the children could describe in rising and falling sound.

● Make a collection of road signs like those below. Let the children draw them on card, cut them out and attach them to thin dowelling or straws. Stand them upright in plasticine. Put two or three in a row and make up a sequence of sound to describe the journey of a car passing the signs. (It would be useful to have more than one STOP sign.)

> **Music corner** – put the signs in the music corner and let the children continue their exploring.

RISING AND FALLING STEP BY STEP

Granny came to our house

VC

Gran - ny came to our house, she was - n't ve - ry well, She had to stay in bed and rest her knee._____ Twen - ty times a day you would hear my gran - ny say, 'Bring me up a nice hot cup of tea'. And I'd go, '1, 2, 3, 4, 5, 6, 7, 8, Here's your tea.'

This song emphasises step-by-step movement. Ask a child to pick out the bracketed notes on a xylophone. Can he or she bring the grandchild back down the stairs?

Using tuned percussion

Up or down

Ask the children to listen while you play each note of a xylophone (C – C′) from low to high. They can either stand up as you play or raise one hand into the air. Now play from high to low. The children should sit down or lower their hands.

●What do the children notice about the length of the bars in relation to their pitch?

●Mix up rising and falling patterns.

Staircase games

These games use sound to describe the physical act of going up and down stairs. Use a xylophone or other pitched percussion with the notes C D E F G A B C′.

Make two staircase cards:

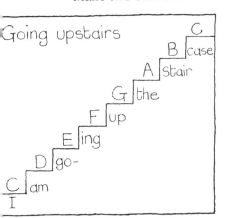

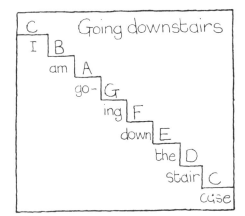

●First sing and play on the xylophone – 'I am go-ing up the stair-case' starting on low C. Invite the children to join in the singing, and make a rising hand movement.

●Now sing and play 'I am go-ing down the stair-case'.

●How else could they go up or down the stairs? – running, creeping, stamping, tip-toeing, as though tired, angry, sad, etc. How would the children sing and play in each case?

●Ask a child to point to the steps as they are played.

Mini-stories with sound

In pairs the children can play and say these mini-stories together. One child tells the story, the other makes appropriate instrumental sounds to describe what has happened.

Boma was lying on the bed waiting for Claire to come and play. The doorbell rang. Boma jumped off the bed and ran downstairs to answer the door. Halfway down she realised she had forgotten to bring her new car with her, so she ran back, picked up the car and ran back downstairs.

Sharon was playing hospitals with her teddy when Dad called her downstairs to set the table. Sharon was enjoying the game and didn't want to stop. Dad called again, and this time he sounded cross. Slowly Sharon took off her stethoscope and stamped downstairs.

Music corner – let the children use the staircase cards in the music corner. Play these games in pairs:

●One child plays either the upstairs or downstairs tune. The partner listens and points to the card which has been played.

●After some practice, the player can reduce the number of steps climbed, always starting either at the very top or the very bottom, and the listener can point to the number of steps which were played.

●One child indicates by pointing to one of the cards what he or she wants to hear.

STEPS AND SLIDES – *photocopiable gamesheet*

The pictures on the gamesheet show someone or something moving physically up or down. Talk with the children about the pictures. What would be a more appropriate accompanying sound – step-by-step or slide? Think about speed and volume. Which instrumental or vocal sound would they choose for each scenario?

Let the children experiment individually in the music corner with a range of instruments.

Steps and slides

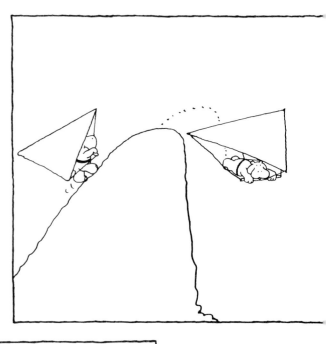

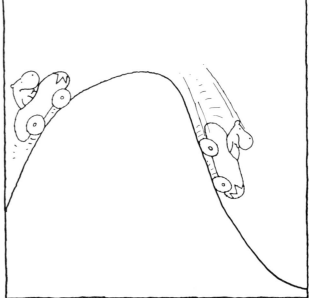

4 More melodic movement

This unit will help the children to develop a more subtle awareness of pitch.

STAYING THE SAME

Exploring

Ask the children to listen out for sounds which stay at the same pitch – the whine of a hair drier, the bleeps of digital alarms, kitchen timers, telephones, some door bells, computer hum, etc. Imitate the sounds with voices and instruments, and draw the sounds in the air. Some of the sounds are continuous, others are repeated.

Singing together

Sing the opening words of these songs. Ask the children to draw a horizontal line in the air when they hear a part of the tune which stays on or repeats the same pitch. Show the children the notation and see if they can spot where the pitch stays the same.

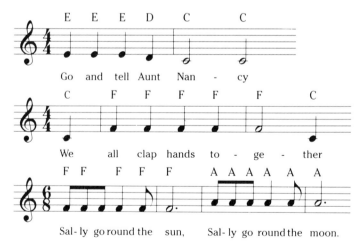

> **Music corner** – write out the opening words of the tunes onto cards and let the children try to pick them out by ear on a xylophone (C – C′). Let them try playing from the music as well.

Copycat

This is a game for two children. Prepare two xylophones by removing all but the same two bars from each (e.g. leaving C and G on each instrument). The two players sit with a screen between them. One player taps one of the two bars and the second player has to tap the same bar on his or her instrument. They can check by looking. Then the second player has a turn. When they are confidently recognising the notes add a third bar

●To make the game even more advanced let the children make up short sequences of notes for their partners to copy.

C E G or E C G G

UP AND DOWN JUMPS

Exploring

Talk about up and down jumps in pitch which the children hear in their environment, e.g.
in computer games, birdsong, sirens and fancy car horns, some door bells.

●Can the children imitate any of these sounds with their voices. Encourage them to link the sounds to body or arm movements as well. Draw the sounds in the air, or stand up, jump and crouch.

Think of situations in which people, animals or things physically move up and down, e.g.
– one or more children on a trampoline
– one or more bouncing balls
– one or more kangaroos
– hailstones bouncing off a tin roof

●Ask the children to use their voices and pitched percussion to describe any of these.

●How rapidly would the sounds occur? How loud or quiet? Would they be regular or random? What would the quality of the sound be like – harsh, muffled, etc?

●Ask the children to draw the sounds in the air with their hands, and then on paper.

Signs and signals

For this you need a xylophone, a screen, and some pieces of paper and crayons. Behind the screen play a two-note jump – either up or down. Invite a child to draw the leap on paper. It might look like this:

If the child draws the second note vertically above the first, play it back sounding the two notes together as the score would imply. Ask the children what needs to be done to make the score more accurate i.e. the second note needs to be drawn to the right of the first to show that it follows sequentially.

The listening children can draw the jump in the air. Talk about the jump – did it go up or down? Was it a small or a large jump? (To start with you can make the leaps large and obvious, gradually introducing smaller leaps.) When the children are good at recognising two note jumps, extend them to three notes. The scoring should give a clear indication of up and down melodic movement:

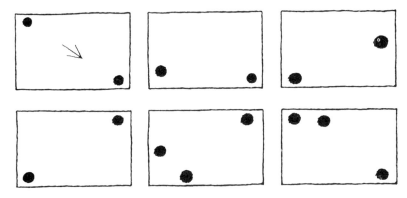

> **Music corner** – make some score cards like these and put them in the music corner with a xylophone. Expect a variety of interpretations. Anything goes as long as it follows the direction of leap indicated by the score.

Singing together

The opening notes of these songs illustrate up and down melodic jumps especially well. Sing them together. Ask the children to describe the melodic movement. Draw the shape of the movement in the air and on paper. Show them the notation.

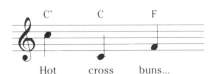

Hot   cross   buns...

Dai - sy,   Dai - sy...

Old   wo - man,   old   wo - man...

Have   you   a - ny   bread   or   wine

> **Music corner** – write the opening words of the songs onto cards and put them in the music corner with a xylophone. Can the children pick out the notes of the tunes by ear? Some children may also like to play from the music as it is written here (the letter names will help them).

COMBINING SLIDES, STEP-BY-STEP, LEAPS, AND STAYING THE SAME

The following activities make the link between high and low pitch and high and low movement.

Sound signals

You will need space to play this. Prepare a xylophone with the notes C – C'. Ask the children to listen to the xylophone and do what it 'says'. If they hear a quick upwards slide, they should stand up quickly and smoothly, a slow step-by-step descent means lower yourself bit by bit to the floor. A repeated low note means crawl around on the floor, a repeated in-between note means walk normally, a repeated high note means move around on tiptoe stretching high. When they hear a lot of jumps from low C to high C' and back, they can touch toes and stretch in the air over and over until the signal stops.

●Let the children suggest other signals.

Mini-stories with sound

Ask the children to make up some xylophone music to go with each of these mini-stories. Talk about each one and decide if it would be best to start playing with a high note, a low note or an in-between note. Think about tempo, volume, rhythm and melodic direction.

> The man was in a hurry. As the crossing gates were closed he had to use the footbridge over the railway line. He ran quickly up the steps, across the bridge and down the other side.
>
> The rabbit hopped around nibbling the grass. Suddenly it lifted its nose and sniffed. Fox! Quick as a flash it ran down its burrow to safety.
>
> The horse had two jumps left to go. It galloped up to the first and jumped up and over to the other side. At the second jump the horse skidded to a halt. It's rider trotted it round and this time the horse jumped clear over. On it galloped to the finish. Tired it trotted away to rest.

> A jogger is running along a level road. She starts to climb a hill. It's a long hill and she gets tired and slows down. At the top the road levels out again and the jogger picks up speed and runs off into the distance.
>
> The swimmer ran along the high diving board and dived into the water below.

Signs and signals

Draw simple scores to go with the stories. The last might look like this:

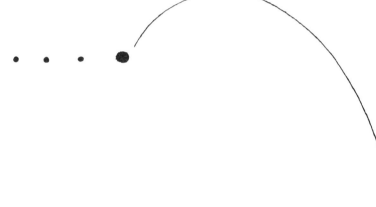

HUNT THE NOTE – *photocopiable gamesheet*

What you need:
Two players each with two beaters
Two pitched percussion instruments each prepared with the eight notes C to C'
A screen (or players sit back to back)
Two copies of the gamesheet – one per child

To play:
One player is the leader, the other copies him or her. The leader can choose to play any of the patterns on the gamesheet, and the follower must listen, find the pattern on the sheet, and play it back.

Hunt the note

The science of sound – *higher and lower*

The three main factors affecting pitch are *length*, *size*, (or mass) and *tension*. The pitches produced by musical instruments are usually influenced by a combination of all three.

Why are some sounds higher or lower than others?

Fast vibrations produce high notes, slow vibrations produce low notes. The speed of vibrations is called the *frequency*. Mass, length and tension all affect frequency. A long, loose, thick string produces a low note, whereas a short, tight, thin string produces a high note. It is difficult to *see* any differences in speed of vibrations except on the strings of large, stringed instruments such as the guitar or 'cello. Children might be able to see frequency variations on rubber bands or a twanged ruler.

Size or mass

Voices

Which children in your group have noticeably high voices and which have noticeably low voices? Compare the heights of the two sets of children. Is there any relationship between size and voice type? You will probably find that some of your high-pitched children are small and some of the children with low voices are big. This won't always be the case. Make a Carroll diagram to show your findings.

	big	small	
		Tina Katie Mark	high voices
	Tom Cara Leon	Tony	low voices

The pitch of your voice depends on the size of your larynx or voice box. People with deep voices have large larynxes, people with high voices have small larynxes.
●Why do boys' voices often get deeper as they get older? Boys' voices 'break' as their voice boxes grow. Girls go through a similar stage, but the difference in pitch isn't so dramatic because the physical change isn't so great.

Instruments

Collect a few earthenware plant pots of different sizes and suspend with rope from a rail. Tap each and listen carefully to the sound produced. Which ones produce the higher sounds?

Make a collection of triangles of different sizes. Arrange in order of size. Tap each in turn. Is there a difference in pitch? Which ones produce the lowest sounds?

If possible compare the size and sound of a violin and a 'cello, a descant and a treble recorder, an alto and a bass xylophone.

Length

The children have already considered the length of bars on pitched percussion instruments in relation to their pitch (see page 59). There are several simple experiments which demonstrate this principle:

●Slowly pour coloured water into a tall, thin transparent container. Listen to the sound as the container fills up. It gets higher because the vibrating column of air at the top of the utensil gets shorter as the water rises.

●Put varying amounts of water in five (or more) milk bottles. Gently tap the bottles to produce a sound. Why are some sounds higher than others?

●On a stringed instrument such as a guitar, show the children what happens when you shorten the length of the vibrating string. If you look inside a piano you will see the strings of different lengths. Look at a picture of a harp.

Tension

Tension is the third main factor determining the pitch of a sound. If you have a drum or tambour with tuning screws, show the children how tightening the skin results in a higher sound, and slackening the skin produces a lower sound. You can demonstrate this on a guitar or any other stringed instrument by tightening and slackening the strings. How is a piano tuned? Experiment with rubber bands to produce higher and lower sounds. Singers who are nervous and tense sometimes sing a bit sharp because their vocal chords tighten up.

Is it possible to measure pitch?

Yes, but it is unlikely that a school would have the instruments necessary to do this. Ask the school nurse to demonstrate how he or she conducts hearing tests with an audiometer. Pitch is usually measured in number of vibrations per second. Most people can hear between 20 and 20,000 vibrations per second.

1 Long and short in contrast

Exploring

Talk about sounds which go on for a long time (in music they are called sustained sounds). Reproduce the sounds with either the real thing or a vocal imitation. Here are some ideas:

– *School*: the murmur of voices, playground noise, a large piece of paper slowly ripped in two, fire alarm, scraped chair, bell.

– *Home*: door bell (pressed for a long time), vacuum cleaner, hair dryer, washing machine spin, running tap, kitchen timer, humming fridge, cat purring, dog growling.

– *Outside*: aeroplane, vehicle engine, drumming rain, roll of thunder, siren, fog horn, bleat of a sheep, low of a cow, bee buzzing, splashing through paddling pool.

●Which of these are one sustained sound, and which are a sustained sound made up of a lot of shorter sounds, e.g. applause or a drum roll.

Talk about sounds which are very short. Reproduce the sounds with the real thing or a vocal imitation of it.

– *School*: the sound of a child making a dotty pattern with crayons, the snip of a pair of scissors, footsteps in the corridor, the bleeps in some computer games, tapping the keys of a typewriter or computer keyboard, the tap of a hammer.

– *Home*: tick of a clock, bark of dog, bleep of a digital alarm, coughs and sneezes, drip of tap, click of a switch.

– *Outside*: chirp of sparrow, click of car indicator, horses' hooves, tap of woodpecker, footstep on concrete, bleep on pelican crossing, chopping of wood.

●Talk about and compare the long and short sounds you have been exploring. What is the longest sound the children have ever heard, or can thing of? What is the shortest sound they have heard or can think of?

●Can any of the sounds you have been discussing be *made* longer, or shorter? Choose one and imitate it vocally in this sequence –

SHORT   IN-BETWEEN   LONG

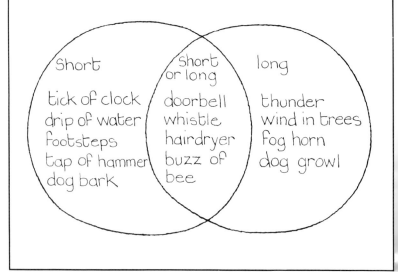

Music corner – Make a Venn diagram of long and short sounds, and in the intersection of the circles put those sounds which can be made either long or short. Display it in the music corner, where the children can imitate the sounds with their voices or bodies.

Short | Short or long | long
tick of clock | doorbell | thunder
drip of water | whistle | wind in trees
footsteps | hairdryer | fog horn
tap of hammer | buzz of bee | dog growl
dog bark | |

Signs and signals

Make up hand signs together to indicate whether a sound should be sustained or very short, e.g.

Vocal sounds

Who is tapping at my window?

'Who is tapping at my window?'
   'It's not I,' said the cat.
   'It's not I,' said the rat.
   'It's not I,' said the wren,
   'It's not I,' said the hen.
   'It's not I,' said the fox.
   'It's not I,' said the ox.
   'It's not I,' said the dog.
   'It's not I,' said the frog.
   'It's not I,' said the hare.
   'It's not I,' said the bear.
'It is I,' said the rain,
'Tapping on your window pane.'

● Compare the hiss of a snake, the howl of a wolf, the buzz of a bee, and the lowing of cows with the squeaks of guinea pigs and mice, the chirp of sparrows and grunts of pigs.

● Can the children think of animals which can produce both long and short sounds? Imitate the purring of a cat and it's angry spit, the long growling and short yelp of a dog.

● Sit in a circle and say the poem together. At the end of each line, pause and point to a child to imitate the animal's sound. Everyone can help to make a rain sound at the end.

Mary rose

Mary Rose sat on a pin.

Ahhhhhhhhhhh!

Mary rose.

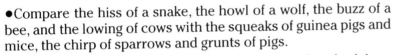

● Sit in a circle and chant the rhyme together. Each person takes a turn to provide the anguished scream. Alternate between long and short screams. Choose a conductor to direct the length of the scream.

Balloon

Suck in some air,
Push it all out.
Do it again,
Watch it grow stout.
Bigger and bigger –
Soon you must stop.
Careful, be careful,
It's going to POP!

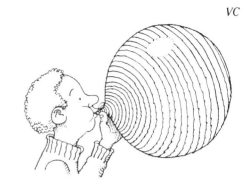

● Ask the children to pretend to blow up a balloon as you are reading them the poem; suck in quickly after lines 1, 3, 5, 7, blow out slowly after lines 2, 4, 6, 8. This will make a short/long sequence of sounds.

● Let everyone clap on the loud POP at the end.

Drip drop

Here a drip,
There a drop,
Everywhere a drip drop.

Here a pitter,
There a patter,
Everywhere a pitter patter.

Now a heavy, steady thrumming.
Listen to the water drumming.

● Sit in a circle and practise making raindrop sounds with voices and body sounds – find an appropriate combination of sounds for each stanza.

● Choose a leader to say the poem, and divide the others into three groups – one for each stanza. After the first verse the leader pauses and the first group makes their sounds. They continue while the second stanza is recited. Pause again while the second group join in with their sound, and so on.

● A fourth listening group can raise their hands at the point when they hear that the rain sounds have become sustained.

When I go to bed

VC

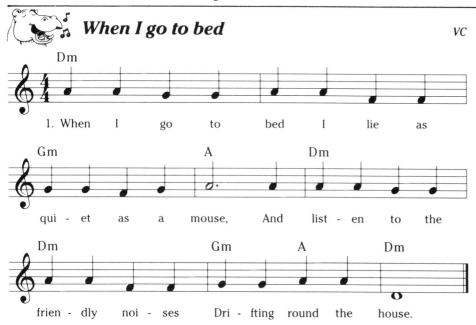

1. When I go to bed I lie as

qui - et as a mouse, And list - en to the

frien - dly noi - ses Dri - fting round the house.

2 The far-off sound of talking and the creaking of the floor,
Music from the radio, the banging of a door.

3 The sound of people's footsteps as they walk along the street,
Clicks and creaks and rumbles as the radiators heat.

4 Cups and saucers clinking as they're washed and put to dry.
Barking dogs and yowling cats, the buzzing of a fly.

5 The rumbling sound of traffic and a sudden noisy laugh,
Splashing from the bathroom as my sister has a bath.

● Talk about the sounds the song mentions – are they long or short? Talk about volume and pitch as well.

● Either pause at the end of the verse to imitate the sounds, or build an accompaniment of them which some of the children could play quietly in the background as the others sing the song.

Instrumental sounds

Set out a collection of untuned school percussion instruments – maracas, a triangle, coconut shells, a woodblock, Indian bells, a large cymbal, a drum, a tambour, guiro, claves and tambourine. Let the children experiment to find ways of making long and short instrumental sounds.

● Explore techniques for producing short sounds on each of the instruments, e.g. tapping a woodblock or tambourine.

● Now explore techniques for producing long sounds on each of the instruments, e.g. rubbing the woodblock with its beater or with a finger nail, or shaking a tambourine.

● Which instrument produced the longest sound (in some cases the sound can be made to go on indefinately, e.g. rubbing the fingertips round the skin of a tambourine)? Which produced the shortest sound?

● Use the sounds you have explored to accompany the poems and song in this unit.

STARTING AND STOPPING – *photocopiable gamesheet*

This game will help the children get accustomed to starting a sound together and stopping after a given length of time. Before putting the game in the music corner, play it with the whole class, letting individual children take turns to conduct. You will need to draw larger versions of the pictures on a sheet of paper, or a blackboard.

Decide together on an appropriate vocal sound for each picture, and conduct by moving a pointer along one of the pictures. The sound continues for as long as the pointer is touching the picture. Move the pointer from left to right, and vary the speed.

Put copies of the gamesheet in the music corner, and let the children play in pairs, taking turns to play and conduct. They can use instrumental sounds instead of vocal sounds. Encourage them to make up their own pictures.

Starting and stopping

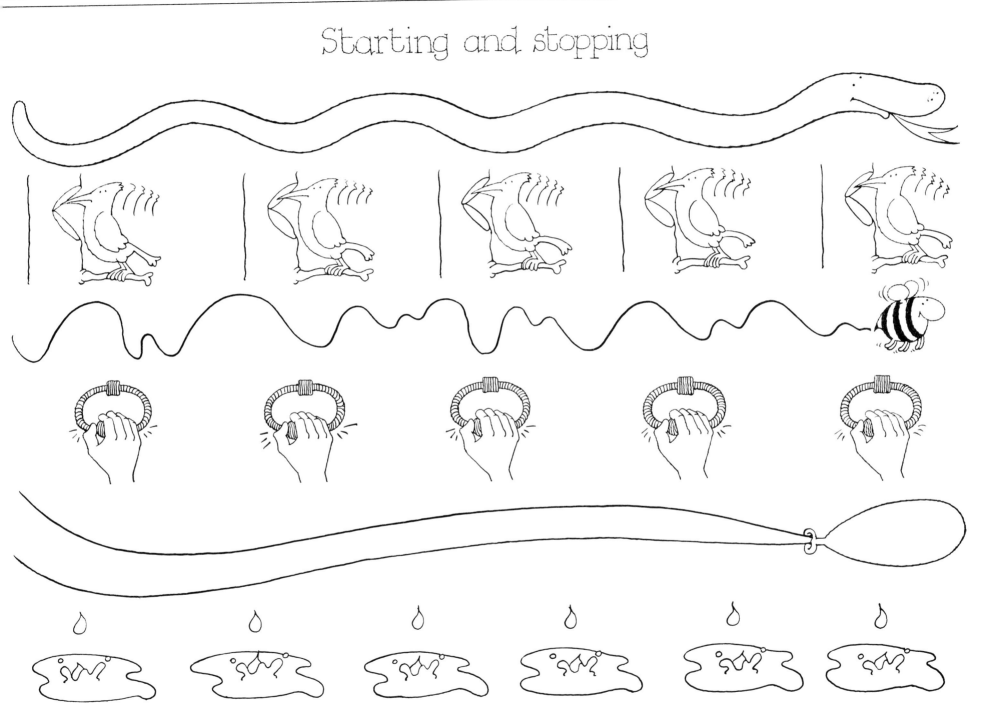

2 Long and short in sequence

This unit takes the sounds explored in unit one and extends them into sequences.

Exploring

Talk about occasions when a long sound is followed by a short sound or vice versa, e.g.

– you are running the water for a bath. You turn off the tap but it keeps dripping for a short while then stops.

– an alarm clock ticks away quietly, then loudly rings.

– coming down a water slide, you scream then SPLASH! you land in the water.

– one minute to midnight. The grandfather clock ticks solemnly away then slowly chimes twelve times.

– mum's making a bird table. First she saws then she hammers.

Use voices or instruments to imitate some of these sequences, e.g.

Running water – tambourine or maraca shaken continuously
Dripping tap – woodblock tapped randomly

●Let pairs of children take turns to perform sequences, and let the listening children discuss the results and offer suggestions for improvement. Make scores of the sequences.

●Draw attention to the fact that short sounds may have very long gaps between them, e.g. a very slowly dripping tap. The gaps may be regular or irregular, e.g. clock ticking – regular, dripping tap – irregular.

●Conversely, long sounds may have a short gap between them, e.g. chiming clock.

Exploring vocal and instrumental sounds

The small ghostie

Barbara Ireson

When it's late and it's dark
And everyone sleeps . . . shhh shhh shhh,
Into our kitchen
A small ghostie creeps . . . shhh shhh shhh.

We hear knockings and raps
And then rattles and taps,

Then he clatters and clangs
And he batters and bangs,

And he whistles and yowls
And he screeches and howls . . .

So we pull up our covers over our heads
And we block up our ears
And we STAY IN OUR BEDS.

●Read this poem and talk about which sounds might be short (knockings, raps, taps), and which might be long (whistles, yowls, screeches, howls, clangs).

●Can any of the sounds be made longer or shorter?

●Use voices and instruments to imitate the sounds. Write out the poem on a large card and let the children play the sounds as you point to the sound words one after the other.

Long jump

VC

Preparation,	Increase the speed,
Concentration.	Faster, faster,
Deep, slow breathing.	Body freed –
Eyes ahead,	J U M P
Body tense.	And land,
Shoulders heaving, then . . .	Feet first,
Start to run.	In sand.

●Talk about the long and short sounds.

●Perform the poem in sound alone.

●Ask the children to draw a score of the sounds.

Johnny get your hair cut

1. John - ny, get your hair cut, snip, snip, snip, snip,

John - ny, get your hair cut, snip, snip, snip.

Johnny chop the firewood . . .

Johnny kick the football . . .

Johnny sound the hooter . . .

Johnny heat the popcorn . . .

Johnny click your fingers . . .

Johnny put the light on . . .

Johnny type a letter . . .

Johnny start the engine . . .

Add actions and sound effects using anything handy and effective – instruments, voices, body sounds or whatever. Decide together whether the sounds should be short or long, single or repeated, random or regular. Can the children hear any silences?

●Choose a child to make a pattern out of one of the sounds from the song for the others to copy e.g.

snip snip — chop pop — | snip snip — chop pop —

Follow on

Distribute a set of instruments with resonant sounds among a group of children and sit the players in a circle. Ask the children to tap their instruments in turn, playing only when the sound of the previous instrument *has completely faded away*. Do the same with the instruments which produce a shorter sound. What do the children notice about the frequency of tapping? Another time try with a mixture of instruments.

Sound and silence

Ask two children to select an instrument each and go behind a screen. Ask one child to play a short sound, and the other to play a long sound. Let them take it in turns to play. Can the others, with closed eyes, draw a horizontal line in the air to match the duration of the sound they hear, and put their fingers on their noses during the silences between sounds. The playing children can have fun drawing out the gaps or making them very short.

Signs and signals

●Decide together on a sign and hand signal to indicate a rest.

READING LONG AND SHORT *– photocopiable gamesheet*

Here the children are asked to play from a simple instrumental score. Each piece is made up of long and short sounds. The sustained sounds are depicted by long symbols. The short sounds are drawn as small, compact shapes. The players don't have to conform to a standard beat or pulse, but they should tap or shake or scrape as many times as there are symbols. They should be guided by the length of the symbol as to the duration of the sound and by the space between the symbols as to the duration of a silence.

The players can use their own judgement in this or be guided by a conductor. To conduct the music point to each symbol in turn.

The first page is for just one player and one instrument. A variety of techniques will be required for playing the instrument to produce both long and short sounds, e.g. the tambourine will have to be shaken and tapped.

The second page is for two players and two instruments.

Reading long and short (one player)

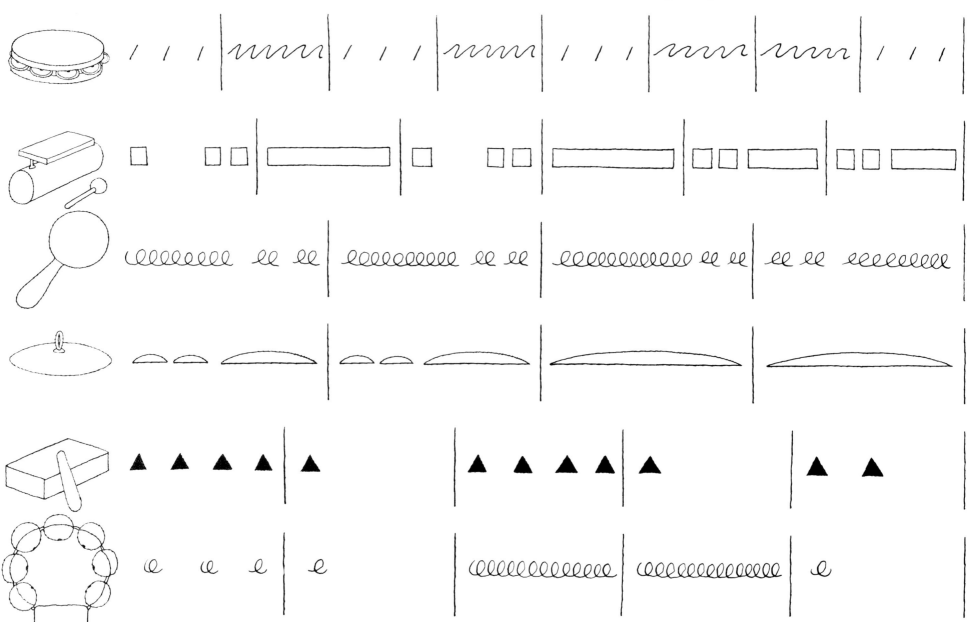

Reading long and short (two players)

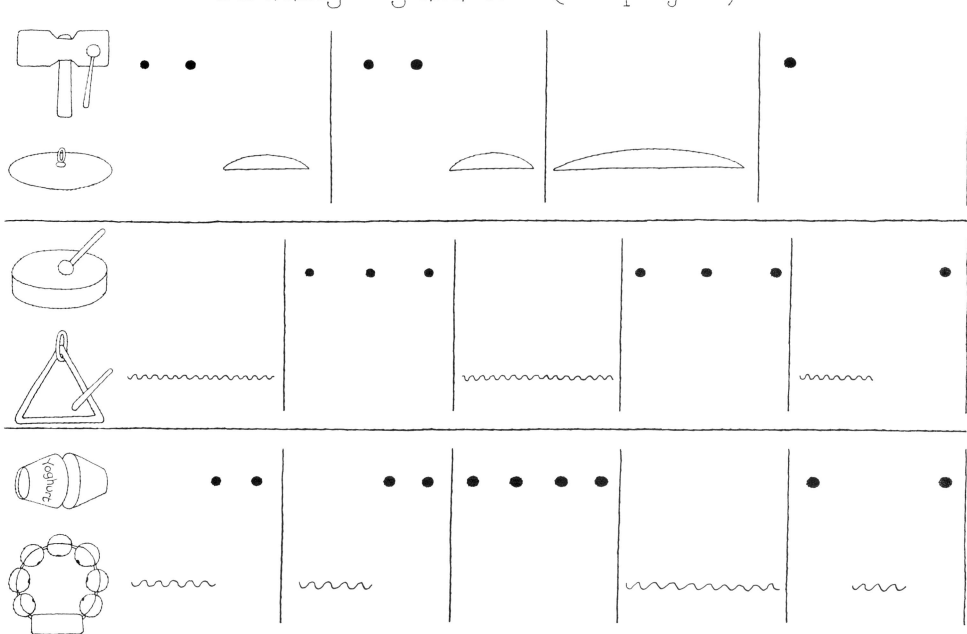

3 Long and short together

In the previous two units the children have talked about and reproduced a variety of sustained and short vocal and instrumental sounds. They have played them on their own and in sequence. Here they are encouraged to play longer and shorter sounds at the same time. The sounds are not controlled by a beat or rhythm as in the next unit, but instead are fairly random.

Exploring

Talk about situations like those below where long and short sounds are heard together. Use voices, bodies and instruments to reproduce the sounds. Copy the scores onto a large sheet of paper. Divide into two groups – one for each sound and conduct them by moving a pointer along the score from left to right.

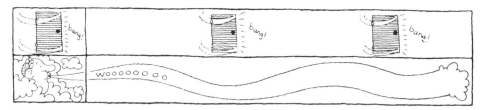

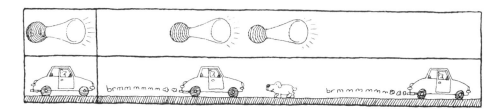

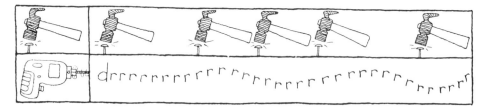

●Ask the children to make up their own sequences.

Instrumental and vocal sounds

Bubble bubble bubble

Bubble, said the kettle,
Bubble, said the pot,
Bubble, bubble, bubble,
We are very, very hot.

Long – chant the jingle against a quiet background of continuous bubbling sounds – either use voices or blow through straws into water.

Short – ask a few children to pretend to chop up vegetables to go into the boiling water – use woodblocks, rulers tapped on table tops, vocal clicks or chant 'chop chop'. The choppers need make no attempt to keep together. They can chop quickly or slowly, in fits and starts with rests between.

Long and short together – Put the continuous bubbling and the chopping sounds together, and chant the jingle against the cooking sounds.

●Ask the children in pairs to make up a score like those opposite to show the bubbling and chopping sounds. Swap and play back each others score.

Hark, hark, the dogs do bark

Hark, hark, the dogs do bark,
The beggars are coming to town.
Some in rags, and some in tags,
And one in a velvet gown.

Long – snarls and growls

Short – yaps and snaps, tapping of footsteps.

Long and short together – divide into four groups – one to snarl and growl, another to yap and snap, a third to make the sound of footsteps, and the fourth to chant the rhyme to the accompaniment of the others.

●Make scores in pairs as above.

Engineers (extract)

Jimmy Garthwaite

Pistons, valves and wheels and gears,
That's the life of engineers.
Thumping, chunking engines going,
Hissing steam and whistles blowing.

Talk about engines and the sounds and movements they make. Divide your group into four and allocate a sound and movement to each, e.g.

Group 1 – make thumping movements with fists to an accompaniment of soft regular thuds on drums or tambours.

Group 2 – make a roly-poly hand action to the accompaniment of a vocal hiss, supplemented with shakers.

Group 3 – make sudden jerks to an accompaniment of metallic clanks on triangles and small cymbals.

Group 4 – make whistling sounds vocally or with recorder tops or party blowers. They can be random or regular.

●Look for a variety of volume.

●Appoint a conductor to bring each group in one at a time until the machinery is in full swing. The conductor can create pauses in the music by stopping the machinery and starting it up again.

●Read the poem against this exciting background of sound.

Is anyone home?

VC

Claire and Beth had kicked their ball over into Mr and Mrs Adams' garden. They went round to try to get it back. Claire rang on the front door bell . . . No answer. The children knew someone was in because they could hear the television. Beth rang the bell this time – even longer . . . Still no answer. Beth said she'd go round and knock on the back door. She knocked loudly . . . No-one heard.

'You ring and I'll knock,' shouted Claire. And Beth called back,

'Ready, steady, go!' . . .

After a few moments of ringing and knocking the girls decided to give up. As they were walking away down the path, Mr Adams appeared at the front door. 'Hello,' he said, 'I thought I saw someone walk past the window. Have you kicked the ball over again?'

Provide sound effects for this story.

Singing together

These songs and their very simple accompaniments combine the long sustained sounds of the tuned percussion or recorders with the melody line made up or shorter sounds. When the children know the songs well, clap or tap on woodblocks the rhythm of the melody against the sustained accompaniment of tuned percussion.

The farmer's in his den

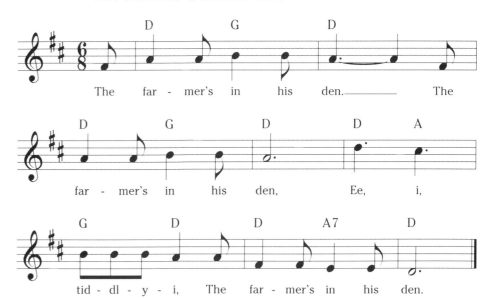

Tuned percussion or recorder – play throughout.

Hickory dickory dock

Hick - o - ry dick - o - ry dock,_____ The

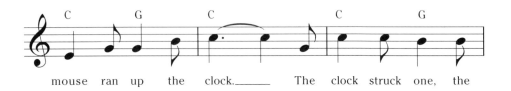

mouse ran up the clock._____ The clock struck one, the

mouse ran down. Hick - o - ry dick - o - ry dock.

Tuned percussion or recorder – play throughout.

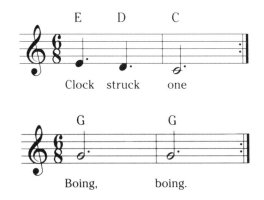

Clock struck one

Boing, boing.

The Terrible Boggart

VC

In this story the children can have fun combining animal sounds – both their voices and sound of their feet – and engine noises. Tell the children the story then go back and look at the places where there are asterisks. What sort of sound combinations would be heard at these points? Imitate them with voices, bodies and instruments and tell the story again, this time adding the sounds.

Life at Buttercup Farm had been quite pleasant until the day the Terrible Boggart, (or TB, as he was known to his enemies), came to live under the bridge that spanned the babbling brook.

It wasn't just his smell – that was bad. It out-ponged the midden in the farmyard. And it wasn't just his looks. After all, he couldn't really help the huge, hairy warts that covered his nose or the nasty green colour of his skin. No – it was EVERYTHING about him. He was rude, he was noisy and, worst of all, he seemed to think he owned the bridge. Crossing the bridge became a nightmare for the animals. Every time they approached the bridge, bearing little posies of flowers or jugs of creamy milk – anything to keep the TB happy, they could hear him mumbling and grumbling, 'Who's that? What's yer name?' Where yer goin'?' 'S'my bridge. Go away'. Unfortunately the animals couldn't go away. The best grazing land lay on the other side of the bridge, so did the duck pond, and there were no other bridges nearby, so the animals had to grit their teeth and make a dash for it.

Now the TB had one big disadvantage, (apart from his smell, his looks and his manners) and that was his eyesight. He was almost blind. So the TB couldn't actually *see* who was crossing his bridge. In order to know who was approaching he would make the animals snort or moo or growl, and they had to keep this up all the time they were on the bridge. So if, for example, the geese wanted to get to the pond, they would paddle up to the pond, feathers all a-tremble, whereupon the boggart would leap out and snarl, 'Halt who goes there?' And the geese would waddle across the bridge hissing like mad ∗. The hens would cluck ∗. The sheep would bleat ∗. The cows would moo ∗. The ducks would quack ∗ and the two farm dogs would bark ∗.

Now all this wouldn't have been too bad if it hadn't been for the nasty habit the TB had of occasionally attacking the animals as they crossed. One day he would have it in for the ducks, the next day it could be the sheep. On Thursday March 15th he was most unpleasant to the hens. They were halfway across the bridge clucking away like the clappers when the TB suddenly decided he didn't like hens, so he leapt out, (giving them a terrible fright) and shoved them all in the water. The hens never left the farmyard after that.

Now there was one thing the Terrible Boggart never challenged and that was the tractor. He was frightened by machinery. He'd once had his hairy big toe run over by a motorbike and since that day had had a healthy respect for anything on wheels. When the tractor approached the bridge there was none of this 'Who goes there?' business. Instead the Boggart would hide under the bridge until the tractor had crossed over, then he would emerge trembling and in a mean mood.

Some of the smaller, more agile animals had the bright idea of hitching lifts on the tractor. The cats and the dogs and the ducks simply hopped aboard and were able to cross the bridge without the TB even knowing they were around.

It was the cows who had the biggest problem. They were too big and too clumsy and too many to get on to the tractor and they simply *had* to cross the bridge to get to the lush green grass in the meadow beyond the bridge. After a series of nasty incidents, including the time the TB sank his sharp teeth into Daisy's rump, the cows decided something would have to be done.

It was Lilac who had the brainwave. 'Look girls,' she said. 'The TB hates tractors. If we could manage to sound like tractors instead of cows we might be able to cross the bridge in safety.'

It took a while for the less intelligent cows to grasp the gist of Lilac's plan, but eventually the penny dropped and soon strange motorised sounds could be heard coming from the cow shed . . . *

Next day at eight o'clock in the morning the cows went out to graze. As they approached the bridge Lilac whispered, 'OK girls, this is it. Get into first gear.'

One by one the cows started revving up *. The troll who was rolling in a cowpat and biting his toe nails looked up startled. One tractor he could cope with but this sounded like a whole battalion. He put his feet over his ears and waited for the noise to go away *. A bit later he crawled out and was particularly unpleasant to the piglets who were unfortunate enough to be playing near the bridge.

From that day onwards life started to look up for the cows. Twice a

day they roared across the bridge in top gear and twice a day the TB shivered and shook under the bridge. Soon the other animals caught on to the idea. The farm cats pretended to be motorbikes *, the sheep pretended to be old bangers *, the pigs pretended to be lorries *, and if they were feeling particularly mean the cows, sheep, cats and pigs would cross together *. Life for the TB began to be unbearable. One moonless night he packed his possessions and sloped off across the fields to find somewhere else to live.

Now, a word of advice to you. If you ever come across a bridge in a lonely spot, just to be on the safe side, make the noise of a tractor or a bus or even an aeroplane as you cross it. You never know – it might just happen to be the day the Terrible Boggart has got it in for little children *.

CROSS THE BRIDGE – *photocopiable gamesheet*

This is a game for three players. One is the conductor, the second makes continuous engine sounds, and the third makes the short sounds of the animals' feet as they cross the bridge.

What you need
- One copy of the gamesheet – cut out the two sets of six cards showing the animals and vehicles
- A stick or pointer
- A selection of instruments

To play:
First the children need to experiment with making animal and engine sounds – they can use voices, body sounds, or instruments (gravel in a margarine tub makes a good engine sound). When everyone is ready, place the cards face down in two piles – one for the animals, the other for the vehicles. The two players turn over the top card of their respective piles. The conductor gives a signal to begin, and slowly moves the pointer over the bridge, while the other two make their combination of sustained engine sounds, and short animal sounds. The sounds stop when the pointer reaches the other side. Turn over two new cards and start again.
- To vary the game, shuffle *all* the cards together before placing them in two piles – this will result sometimes in combinations of just short and short sounds, or just long and long.

The bridge at Buttercup farm

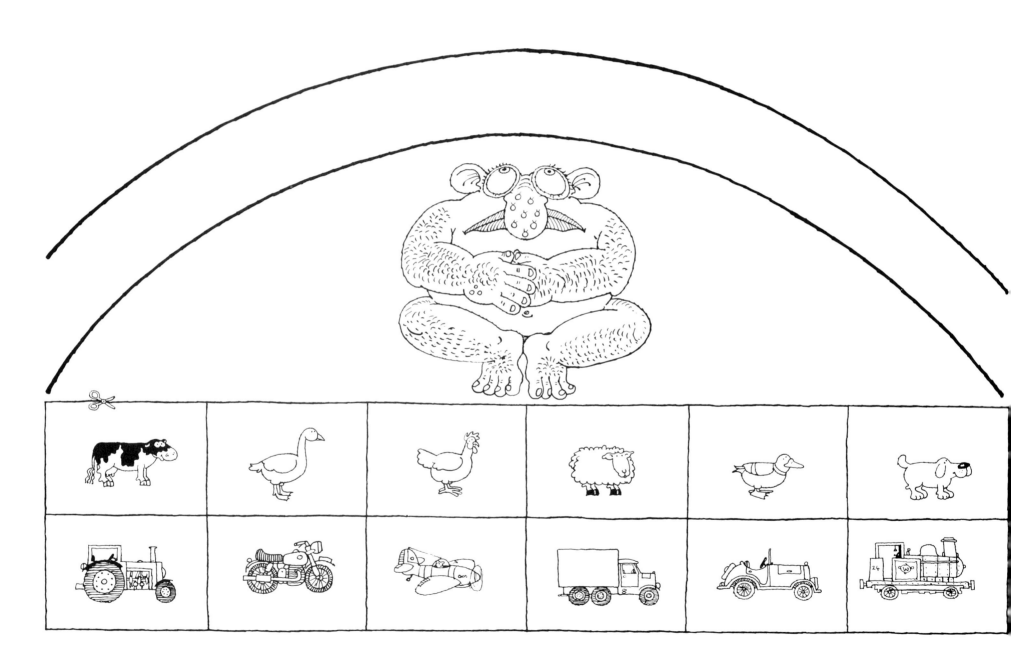

4 Rhythmic patterns

*On hearing a catchy tune, most people will want to clap or tap in time. Some will mark the **beat** (see page 46), some will tap the **rhythm**, some will improvise around both. Whatever they do, they are kept together by the **tempo** of the music (see page 94).*

It is useful for children to be able to recognise and play both the beat and the rhythm of a melody. In the first three units of this section the children experimented with sounds of various lengths. They played them singly, in sequence, and at the same time. In this final unit of the book the children are required to copy the more precise rhythmic patterns created by the words of jingles, songs and chants.

Using action rhymes and songs

Action rhymes and action songs require participants to make a series of movements to match both the meaning and the rhythm of the words. Action rhymes and songs are an excellent preparation for the more precise rhythmic accompaniments suggested later in the unit.

High low dolly pepper

High low dolly pepper, kick kick kick,
High low dolly pepper, flick flick flick,
High low dolly pepper, slap slap slap,
High low dolly pepper, clap clap clap.

●Raise hands and arms high on the first word of each line, lower them on *low*, and make a rocking action on *dolly pepper*. The kicks, flicks, slaps and claps should match the rhythm of the last three words of each line.

Ring the bell

Ring the bell,
Ting-a-ling,
Knock at the door,
Rat-a-tat-tat.
Turn the knob,
Clickety-click.
Walk right in,
'How d'you do?'

●First chant the poem, making actions to match the rhythm of the words in lines two, four and six.

Kangaroo Brown

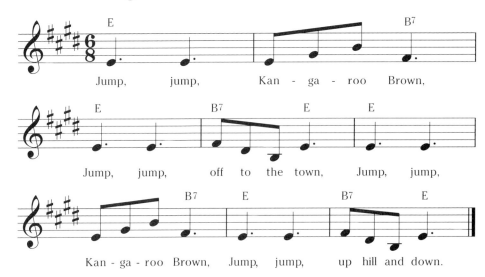

●Slap thighs gently, both hands together, on each *jump*. Clap the rhythm of the words in bars 2, 4, 6 and 8 (four claps each time).

●Find a bouncy sounding instrument for all the jumps, another instrument for the words *Kangaroo Brown*, and a third instrument for the lines *off to the town* and *up hill and down*. The players will have to concentrate hard if they are to play at the right times.

●Play the note B on a pitched percussion instrument for each *jump*.

Wind the bobbin up

Wind— the bo - bin up, Wind— the bob - bin up,

Pull, pull, Clap, clap, pull. Point to the cei - ling,

Point to the floor, Point to the win - dow,

Point to the door. Clap your hands to-ge - ther now,

One two three, Pat them, pat them on your knee.

●Make the actions fit each word and syllable. Clap the rhythm of the repeated *wind the bobbin up*, pull fists apart for each *pull*. The other actions are self-explanatory, but take care to make them match each syllable, i.e. at *point to the window*, point on every syllable not just the first.

Using jingles

Traditional jingles with their well-defined and familiar rhythms provide an excellent starting point for more exacting rhythm work. As some of the words have fairly rapid rhythmic patterns it is a good idea to start slowly and build up speed. Remember to give a clap or tap or shake for every syllable of each word. Explain to the children that you want them to play the rhythm, and ask them to watch you carefully and copy. Look out for those children who persist in playing the beat, and if necessary help them to move their hands in time. One or two children can play the rhythms on instruments. Young children find it easier to tap than shake, so start of with tambours, tambourines, woodblocks and claves.

Further ideas for rhythm work are given in the teaching notes which accompany these jingles. Try them out with other jingles with which you are familiar.

Mrs White

Mrs White
Had a fright
In the middle of the night.
Saw a ghost
Eating toast
Halfway up a football post.

●Tap or slap the rhythm of the words as you chant. Try with one or two instruments. When the children know the jingle well, chant and play against a quiet background of spooky noises. The varied random spooky sounds will contrast well with the precision of the rhythmic chanting and playing.

Danny

Danny
Danny
Don't be blue,
Frankenstein was ugly too.

●Tap or slap the rhythm of the words as you chant. Try with instruments.

Rain rain go away

Rain rain go away,
Come again another day.

●Clap, slap or tap the rhythm of the words with body and instrumental sounds. Set the speed by lightly slapping both hands on thighs. When everyone is joining in, chant the words against the beat. Explain that the beat is like a ticking clock and it keeps on and on the same whatever the voices are saying. Practise the rhythm again. Put the two together. Choose one child to play the beat on a tambour, and once the beat is well established bring in the rest of the group, clapping and chanting the rhythm again. Another time, ask half the group to slap the beat and the rest to clap the rhythm. Try combining beat and rhythm in other jingles, songs and nursery rhythms.

1 2 3 4

1 2 3 4

Mary at the cottage door

5 6 7 8

Mary at the cottage gate

●Practise clapping the rhythm. Divide your group into two, and ask one half to clap and chant the first two lines, and the rest to come in with the third and fourth lines. Choose one child in each group to play an instrument.

●Try this two-part technique in *Polly put the kettle on* (one group per stanza), in *One two buckle my shoe* (one group for the numbers, the other for the rest of each line), and *Tinker tailor* (one word each). A variation of this is to split the rhythmic playing between two contrasting body sounds. For example, clap 1 2 3 4 and lightly slap chest for the second line. Then go back to clapping for 5 6 7 8, and the chest sound for the last line. Try with two contrasting instrumental sounds.

Using nursery rhymes

●Nursery rhymes, because they are so well-known are good for all sorts of rhythm work. One child can play the beat, another can tap out the rhythm while the rest sing. Try the following ideas:

Hickory dickory dock

Hickory dickory dock,
The mouse ran up the clock,
The clock struck one,
The mouse ran down,
Hickory dickory dock.

●Tap the beat on a wooden block (to represent the ticking clock), and clap the rhythm. Keep the tempo slow as there are a lot of notes to clap.

Jack and Jill

Jack and Jill went up the hill
To fetch a pail of water,
Jack fell down and broke his crown,
And Jill came tumbling after.

●Gently slap thighs on the beat with alternate hands to represent Jack and Jill walking up the hill, tap the bouncy rhythm of the words on a wooden block.

The grand old Duke of York

The grand old Duke of York,
He had ten thousand men,
He marched them up to the top of the hill,
And he marched them down again.
And when they were up they were up,
And when they were down they were down,
And when they were only half way up,
They were neither up nor down.

●Tap a solid beat on a drum to represent the marching soldiers, (invite the children to march on the spot in time), and tap the rhythm of the words on a tambourine.

Twinkle twinkle little star

Twinkle twinkle little star,
How I wonder what you are,
Up above the world so high,
Like a diamond in the sky.
Twinkle twinkle little star,
How I wonder what you are.

●Tap a slow beat on a triangle and shake the rhythm of the words with jingle sticks.

Trot trot trot

Trot trot trot, Go and ne - ver
stop, I can ride my lit - tle po - ny,
Though the way is rough and sto - ny, Go and ne - ver
stop, Trot trot trot trot trot.

●Play a regular *clip clop* sound on the beat using coconut shells or a tulip block, and tap out the rhythm on a wood block or jingles or both.

Using rhythms in other chants

Children love playing games with the rhythm of their own names. It is usually more satisfactory to chant both the first name and family name – a first name on its own can sound rather perfunctory. Try the following games:

Pass the tambour (sing to the tune of *London Bridge*)

Pass the tambour round the ring
Round the ring, round the ring.
Pass the tambour round the ring,
Who's the one to tap and sing?

●As the children sing, they pass a tambour (or shaker or jingles) round their circle. Whoever is left holding the instrument on the last word, taps or shakes the rhythm of his or her full name. Repeat until everyone is joining in. Stop and start again.

●Pass two instruments round at the same time. Listen to two name rhythms played at the same time.

●You can make a more extended rhythm by standing two (or more) children side by side and chanting and clapping or playing the rhythms of both their names. Change them round and see if the rhythm has changed. Can anyone make up a tune to the names? Try clapping the names of teachers.

●Clap and play the rhythm of simple sequences: the days of the week, the twelve months, numbers, addresses etc.

What's the tune?

● Children love to play guessing games based on the rhythms of well-known nursery rhymes. Try these. Sing and clap the rhythm of a well-known song such as *Baa baa black sheep*. Then clap the rhythm (no words) to one of the lines, e.g. *Have you any wool* and ask the children to try to identify which bit was clapped.

●Start to clap the rhythm of a well-known song and ask the children to put up their hands as soon as they have identified the song. If they are correct they can chant and play the whole rhythm on an instrument of their choosing.

The science of sound – *longer and shorter*

Instruments

Collect together a range of percussion instruments to include a suspended cymbal, a triangle, a chime bar, Indian bells, a tambour, a maraca, a wood block, a tambourine, a large drum and a xylophone. Allowing just one firm tap or shake per instrument, decide which instruments produce a long (or sustained) sound, and which a short sound. Make two sets and label them (If you like, add a third category of 'in–between'):

Instrument	the vibrating part is made out of –	long sound	short sound
	metal	✓	
	wood		✓

● Which instrument can produce the longest sound? Invite two children to choose an instrument each from the collection of instruments listed above. Say 'ready steady play'. On 'play' each child plays his or her instrument with a firm tap, shake or scrape. Listen to discover which instrument sounds for the longer time. Place the 'winner' on one side. Try again with two different instruments. Again, put the instrument with the longer sound to one side. When all the instruments have been tested, play those instruments which you have set aside off against each other, until an outright 'winner' emerges.

Allsorts

Suspend a variety of objects from a rail using string or cord. The collection could include a cup, two plant pots, (one plastic, one earthenware), a knitting needle, a book, a ruler, a rubber quoit, a bean bag, a fork, a pair of scissors, a sock. Tap each with a rubber beater and record the sounds made on a chart similar to the one below. Which materials are resonant and which are dull?

object	made out of –	resonant	dull
bean bag	cloth and beans		✓
forks	metal	✓	

Sound boxes

Many instruments are constructed around hollow sound boxes.

● Ask the children to look at the school percussion instruments and make a collection of instruments with a hollow part. Their collection might include chime bars, xylophones, glockenspiels, a piano, drums, tulip blocks, tubular wood blocks, bells, maracas. Invite children to put their ears to the sides and back of a piano or guitar and listen while you play.

● What happens if you fill in the hollow parts of instruments?
– Tap an empty biscuit tin. Almost fill it with sand and tap again. What do the children notice?
– Put a thumb over the hole in the tube below the chime bar. Tap the bar. Remove the thumb and tap again. What is the effect of blocking the entrance to the tube? Take a thin piece of card and wiggle it to and fro over the chime bar hole as you play. What is the result? Why?
– Block off the sound holes in a guitar with your hands. Pluck the strings and listen to the sound they produce. Unblock the holes and play again.

Can a long sound be made shorter?

Ask the children to think of ways to stop the sound of a cymbal, e.g. touch the vibrating rim with fingers, a ruler, a foot, a book, a straw. Which is most effective? Why does the sound stop when the rim is touched? Experiment with other instruments in the same way. Record the findings:

Instrument	what I did to stop the sound
	touched the bar
	stopped shaking

Combinations of speed and duration

People tend to associate long notes with slowness and short notes with speed. It is easy and somehow natural to play a slow succession of sounds on a suspended cymbal, and a rapid succession of sounds on a woodblock. Try it the other way round. Ask a child to make the woodblock sound like a slowly dripping tap. Ask a child to make the cymbal sound like a rapidly chiming clock.

Thematic index

INDEX

Poems (titles and first lines)

GLOSSARY OF MUSICAL TERMS

The basic concepts:

Timbre

This word refers to the tone quality of a sound. Timbre is often expressed in terms of colour, texture or even temperature: silvery, warm, rough, dull, bright, mournful, and so on.

Volume

This word refers to the loudness or quietness of sound. Other terms which refer to volume are:

piano (p) – play or sing quietly
forte (f) – play or sing loudly
crescendo (cresc) – a gradual increase in volume. In written music, this sign means crescendo: ◁
diminuendo (dim) – a gradual decrease in volume. In written music, this sign means diminuendo: ▷

Tempo

This refers to the overall pace at which a piece of music is played or sung. The *tempo* or pace can considerably affect the mood of a piece of music – try singing a lullaby first slowly then very quickly.

Pulse or beat

The *pulse* or *beat* can be likened to the ticking of a clock, and as with the ticking of clocks, there are slow beats (grandfather clocks), fast beats (small alarm clocks), and in-between beats (mantelpiece clocks). Beat and tempo are interrelated – music with a fast tempo has a fast beat, music with a slow tempo has a slow beat. Lullabies have a rocking, soothing beat. Marches have a sturdy walking beat which makes you want to walk in time or tap your feet. Most barn dances have a fast beat which makes you want to skip or step in time. In this book the beat is marked / Here is an example:

/ / / /
Twinkle twinkle little star

Rhythm

This refers to the pattern which long and short sounds and pauses make when heard in sequence. Children asked to clap the *rhythm* of a chant or song should give a clap to *every* syllable of every word. When asked to clap the *beat* they should clap the regular 'tick-tock' into which the syllables fall. In this example, the rhythm is marked ✱ and the beat is marked /

/ / / /
Rain rain go a-way
✱ ✱ ✱ ✱ ✱

In written music, rhythm is indicated by notes and rests. In this book the children are asked to find their own ways of recording longer and shorter sounds. They are encouraged to show the duration of the sound or silence by spacing the sounds either near or far apart.

Pitch

This describes the highness or lowness of a sound. It can be helpful to relate sound to physical height – for instance stretching up on tiptoe to indicate a rising pitch – but it can be confusing when very often physically high objects produce low-pitched sounds, e.g. an aeroplane.

In this book the children are asked to find their own ways of recording high, low and in-between sounds. The examples given encourage them to show the relation of one pitch to another by drawing the notes higher or lower on the page, according to their relative pitches. Standard musical notation follows the same principle.

Other terms used throughout the book:

Melody

When rhythm and pitch are combined in a single sequence of sounds the result is melody. It can be sung or played.

Accompaniment

The children are encouraged to build all kinds of accompaniments to the chants, poems, stories and melodies in this book. An accompaniment is a background of sound which relates in some way to the words or melody. This background can take many different forms and the children will have to make all kinds of choices as to its appropriateness – they will have to make decisions about structure (or form) as well as tempo, pitch, timbre, mood, beat and rhythm.

Regular and random

In this book, regular refers to sounds controlled by a common pulse whereas random refers to sounds occurring within a set period of time but not within any controlling pulse. For instance, the children might be asked to create a piece of night music. The sounds need to have a starting and finishing point but within that time, they can occur randomly.

Duration

This refers to the length of time a period of sound or silence lasts.

Sustained

A period of sound or silence which lasts a long time in relation to the other sounds around it.

Staccato

A sound which has an extremely short duration.